Olivier Dupon

# SHOE

## Contemporary Footwear *by* Inspiring Designers

Thames & Hudson

ABOUT THE AUTHOR
Olivier Dupon is an expert in the fields of lifestyle and
fashion. He began his career at Christian Dior, then worked
as a buyer and project manager for several large retail
companies before running his own boutique in Australia for
several years. Now based in London, he scouts international
markets in search of exciting new practitioners of design/
art/craft. His previous books include *The New Artisans*
(2011), *The New Jewelers* (2012), *The New Pâtissiers* (2013),
*Floral Contemporary* (2014) and *Encore! The New Artisans*
(2015), all published by Thames & Hudson. His new book
on luxury jewelry will be published in 2016.

On the cover (front): 'Delaunay' slingback open-toe
sandals in white leather, with signature cut-out wedge
with galvanised gold metal detail, S/S 2015 (carry-over
style), by Charline de Luca. Photo Chiara Giannoni (www.
chiaragiannoni.it); (back) 'Temira' sculpted cage-inspired
stiletto-heeled sock bootie, with velvety black suede straps
interspersed with nude mesh insets, 'Illusion' collection,
F/W 2013–14, by Edmundo Castillo (see p. 108). Photo
Andrea Barbiroli Photography (www.andreabarbiroli.com).

p. 1 'Dequincy' platform low-rise boots in embossed and
printed calfskin, with gold-tipped laces, by Zoe Lee.

p. 2 'Geisha Lines' square-toe ankle-strap pumps in pink,
black and white suede, with hidden platforms and lacquered
sculpted 'Geisha' heels, by Aperlaï.

p. 6 Sketches by Amina Muaddi, aka Oscar Tiye: (from
left to right) 'Niyaf' ankle-strap sandal in red, 'Iman' pump
in gold, and the signature 'Malikah' winged ankle-strap
sandal in red.

*Shoe: Contemporary Footwear by Inspiring Designers*
© 2015 Olivier Dupon

Design by Amélie Bonhomme & Amy Preston
Cover design by Therese Vandling

First published in 2015 in hardcover in the United States
of America by Thames & Hudson Inc., 500 Fifth Avenue,
New York, New York 10110

thamesandhudsonusa.com

Library of Congress Catalog Card Number 2015932449

ISBN 978-0-500-51791-8

Printed and bound in China by Toppan Leefung Printing Ltd

# CONTENTS

Introduction                                              7

THE DESIGNERS

Aga Prus                                                  8
Alejandro Ingelmo                                        14
Aleksander Siradekian                                    22
Allan Baudoin                                            28
Amélie Pichard                                           34
Andreia Chaves                                           42
Aperlaï                                                  48
Aquazzura                                                56
Bruno Bordese                                            66
Burak Uyan                                               74
Charline De Luca                                         80
Chelsea Paris                                            86
Diego Dolcini                                            92
Edmundo Castillo                                        102
Ellen Verbeek                                           110
Ernesto Esposito                                        118
Fred Marzo                                              126
Gio Diev                                                134
Gordana Dimitrijević                                    142
Isa Tapia                                               150
Ivy Kirzhner                                            156
Joanne Stoker                                           164
Kerrie Luft                                             172
Laurence Dacade                                         180
Oscar Tiye                                              188
Paul Andrew                                             194
Rupert Sanderson                                        204
Simona Vanth                                            212
Sophia Webster                                          220
Suecomma Bonnie                                         230
Tabitha Simmons                                         238
Zoe Lee                                                 246

Picture Credits                                         254
Acknowledgments                                         256

At a time when the luxury apparel industry has been struggling to produce steady growth rates, accessories have proven to be a top-performing category. They are generally a lower-priced entry point for customers who wish to own a designer piece but cannot afford the price tag or the lifestyle associated with super-high-end garments. Shoes, in particular, have taken up a sizeable share of the accessories market, and their designers have been propelled to the summit of the fame echelon, sharing the prized spot with the most illustrious names in fashion.

In this saturated field, where even the most historic brands have adopted the 'fast-fashion' model by packing their calendars with more shows and special or pre-season collections, it seems that accessories – and especially shoes – have emerged as an arena that can offer room for experimentation and uniqueness. Whereas clothes are notorious for borrowing from the past, high-fashion shoes are being designed in an age when creative concepts that have not been considered or invented before are a real possibility.

The practical benefits of turning to shoes to offer fresh sartorial highlights include the fact that they present such an easy way to make an outfit look special: simply by switching pairs, one can totally revamp what one is wearing. In addition, since it is almost impossible – in these times of factory-manufactured garments with formatted cuts – to find an outfit that is a perfect fit, luxury hand-stitched shoes can offer a match that is close to ideal. Some companies keep the precise foot imprint of their customers in their archive, so as to provide a service that is almost made-to-measure, while there are fresh-faced designers who have boldly started out their careers by making bespoke creations the cornerstone of their emerging brands, rebelling against an age in which mass-manufacture has become the norm.

These designers are well aware of the emotional, even obsessive connection that shoes can trigger. We might trace this back to a fairy-tale that saw an unhappy young girl live 'happily ever after' thanks to a lost slipper. Cinderella would certainly testify that shoes can change one's life for the better. In reality, they may not have quite such transformative power, but they surely inspire joy and self-confidence, and sometimes envy bordering on lust.

The sensual posture brought about by the arch of a formidable pump; the strut created by strappy heels; the fact that the entire body has to reposition itself in a state of tense balance: high-heeled shoes are literally an extension of the body, and as such they instruct its motion response. All the designers in this book who have mastered the art of the arch have witnessed the transformation while fitting their own customers. Once perched on high heels, women instantly radiate an erotic power.

However, it is no longer just stilettos that are synonymous with 'sexy'. Flats have emerged as formidable contenders, combining assured comfort with femininity. While improved designs mean that show-stopping high heels may also now be supremely comfortable to wear, an increasing number of women are being won over by more pragmatic styles. Some young shoemakers are also creating 'gender-bender' designs that allow women to feel the classic, relaxed elegance of what could pass for men's footwear: not a novelty in itself, but a sign that contemporary shoe designers are able to find a niche attuned to their own aesthetic vision as well as broader market desires.

Luxury shoes cater now more than ever for any occasion, style, fancy or mood, all while asserting their mystique. What might have been categorized as dubious fetishism a few decades ago has developed into a passion that can be openly displayed and shared across the globe in no time, thanks to social media.

The appetite for designs with an individualistic quality has altered the way in which colours, textures and finishes are used, setting the bar sky-high. Add to the revolution in customer expectations the parallel progress made in technology which has helped create new materials and treatments, and it can be affirmed that these are exciting times for high-fashion shoe designers and aficionados alike.

This book gives the chance for up-and-coming as well as established talents to showcase their works – a blend of signature and more recent creations, depending on the designer. The line-up includes names you may recognize and names you may be discovering for the first time. On page after glamorous page, a world of sensuality, modernity and chic is conjured up, complete with glimpses of life behind the scenes.

Some of you will be tempted to add to your footwear collection; others will simply appreciate the technical aspects and novel approaches on display; yet others will be drawn in by tales of the designers' personal trajectories. In the end, I hope that you, too – beguiled by the remarkable creations on show – will succumb to the overwhelmingly seductive quality of master shoemaking.

# AGA
# PRUS

'Simple' is sometimes more difficult to achieve than 'sophisticated'. This is especially so in the world of made-to-measure, where each shoe is created to be the perfect match for its owner through a stringent and costly (in terms of both money and time) process. This back-to-basics approach is all about substance over special effect. That is one reason why made-to-measure has become limited nowadays to men who would rather spend money on a few pairs of long-lasting shoes and women who cannot buy shoes from mainstream shops due to the difficulty of finding a decent fit. This was certainly the state of bespoke shoemaking in Poland before one young woman decided to change the game.

Aga Prus's vision was to revolutionize the world of made-to-order footwear for women by introducing desirability and modernity. Her personal mission: to put her shoemaker grandfather's philosophy back on the map, harking back to a time when made-to-measure shoes were the norm (under the Communist regime many people had no choice but to go to the cordwainer's workshop to buy their shoes, as there was no such thing as proper retail). 'My grandfather, Brunon Kamiński, was originally from a very modest rural background, but he became famous in 1950s Warsaw. His was a true rags-to-riches story. Actresses and in-the-know women formed his loyal clientèle, and he won many awards,' Aga explains. 'He had set up his workshop after the war, having survived the concentration camps. He selected the ground floor of a destroyed building – most of Warsaw having been flattened – where he settled for the rest of his life.' At the peak of his career there were numerous shoe workshops in Warsaw, but today the number has plummeted to around five.

After he died, the business was briefly supervised by Aga's grandmother, but it was eventually taken over by one of her uncles. Her father, despite having been 'raised' in the workshop, opted for a career making windsurfing boards. 'As for me,' says Aga, 'I had no intention of becoming a shoemaker. As a child, I would spend my time with the women in the living quarters on the first floor of the building, whereas the men would be working in the workshop on the ground floor, so really I didn't interact much with the business at the time.'

She decided to study interior design, but quickly realized she did not want to work in that field. She then joined a major graphic design studio, for which she still works as a freelancer. But at some point she felt she wanted to do something for herself. 'It was under my nose all along. I moved to live in the same building where my grandfather's workshop was, so I could smell and touch the lasts every day. For some reason I had been scared of jumping in.' As she recalls, 'I sat down with my father, the one with the shoemaking expertise, and we came up with a plan and our first model, a classic pump. A pump is actually the most challenging product of all, since its shape has to be perfect. It's a very transparent design, with no room for error.'

Aga Prus was born, with Aga at the helm, perfecting the visual branding thanks to her graphic design skills, while her father brought valuable technical prowess. 'I feel like a judge on a panel,' says Aga, 'while my dad is a contractor. I have a precise vision of what I want, and I dictate the direction of Aga Prus.'

The core concept is the creation of a collection that reassures the customer about the type and quality of shoe on offer: the models can all be viewed on the company website or by appointment in person. Following on from the seven styles in two to three colours of her first collection, which she presented at Łódź Fashion Week, Aga now offers some fourteen distinct styles in further colourways. Customers can change these colours altogether, or can choose a different leather; or if the wide range of sizes doesn't suit they can have a shoe altered for a perfect fit; or ultimately they can opt for a brand-new 'from scratch' commission. Options are truly endless. 'If anyone wants something more out of the box, style-wise, it will always be my pleasure to oblige,' adds Aga.

She adds steadily to her initial collection, rather than building an entirely new series each season. 'At the beginning, people were impressed and grateful that a young person would embark on such a challenging project. Some even had memories of their own family going to my grandfather's workshop,' she recounts. 'But building the collection is a slow process, as I struggle to find the time to imagine new designs while having to honour our bespoke shoe orders. Summer time is especially tricky because it's wedding season.'

Aga admits that her own inspiration for bespoke designs is far from 'romantic'. The focus is primarily on ergonomics: 'I think about what would be a good solution for individual feet, and then I try to transfer that into a nice shape and ultimately take into account all of my client's expectations.' Aga points out that, now that she can wear her own products, she can no longer bring herself to buy shoes from shops. 'It's nearly impossible to find nicely shaped shoes, and I'm not even talking about the fit.'

Aga's goal is to change women's perceptions so that they understand that a made-to-measure purchase is a pleasurable one, and a 'luxury' that comes with huge benefits. By successfully fusing ancestral craftsmanship, classic rules, superb materials and modern chic, she has established the foundations of the 'anti-superfluous' concept.

*www.agaprus.pl*

'My motto is that a beautiful shoe should be pure and classic in style, but above all well shaped. Shoes are like sculptures: every line, curve and angle matters. I strive to reconcile style with essential comfort, all the while adding a personal touch.'

(page 8) Aga Prus in her family workshop in Warsaw, holding a photograph of her grandfather Brunon Kamiński (on the right) in front of his collection of lasts.

(this page) Working on the sole for a pair of platform-heeled Chelsea boots.

(opposite) 'Forget-me-not' classic pump in leather.

(opposite, clockwise from top left) **Flat Chelsea boot** in black leather with hidden rubber wedge; **Derby shoes** in brown leather with gold details; **asymmetric peep-toe sandals** in leather with a stripe across both feet; **Derby shoes** in mint leather with silver details; **Derby shoes** in black patent leather with gold details.

(this page, clockwise from top left) **'Minnie' ankle-strap pumps** in leather, designed for Disney's 'Minnie: A Style Icon' project; **'Mokasynka'**, an original fusion of loafers and classic moccasins, here in python and red leather; **flat Chelsea boots** in light brown leather with hidden rubber wedges; **platform-heeled Chelsea boots** in black leather with mixed leathers; **retro chic pumps** in black leather, with insets on each heel and side.

ALEJANDRO

INGELMO

Delicate and sexy, or urban and sporty? With Alejandro Ingelmo's collections, you can be the complete, multi-faceted self that most of us are. A modern, slightly techno aesthetic runs through all his footwear, from the ultra-feminine to the more unisex, so that whether you are wearing strappy stilettos to a chic appointment or a pair of trainers on an urban errand you will maintain the same allure. Alejandro is himself a case in point: he usually sports urban athletic outfits, unless he is attending an event, in which case he puts on a classic slim-fitted suit.

'When it comes to designing shoes, my signature style always remains at the heart of what I do, but I have steadily evolved towards a modern and geometric direction,' he says. 'I'm especially fond of metallic and iridescent materials that give off different effects when the light hits them. These materials have been important to me from the beginning of my career and, thanks to new advances in leather treatments, they have also evolved so that I've been able to procure sexy, geometric and timeless shoes since 2006, the year I officially launched my brand.' One unique marker of Alejandro's work is the graphic toecap that appears on his trainers: two flat insets that contrast with the main body and look somehow futuristic.

His more feminine and sassy styles, on the other hand, evoke Latin sophistication and Caribbean sensuality. A Cuban-American, Alejandro has a family history that helps to shed light on his trajectory. As with many migrant stories, his origins were an indicator and facilitator of things to come. His great-grandfather started out as a cobbler in Salamanca, Spain, but decided to move to Cuba. There he launched Ingelmo Shoes, which, Alejandro relates, soon became the most prestigious men's shoe company in the country. When Fidel Castro came to power, the family moved to Miami, where Alejandro was born and raised. He went on to study shoe and fashion design at Parsons in New York.

'Shoes are literally in my blood. As a fourth-generation shoemaker, I was exposed to shoe design from early on. Creating, developing concepts, and seeking to create an emotional effect and response from my customers is what drives me,' he states. A few years ago, *ELLE* magazine ran a story on Alejandro and the assignment took place in Cuba. 'It was my first time there, and I was able to visit where my family's shoe factory was and where they used to live. It was a very special trip.' Indeed, the shoe store his grandfather owned in Cuba inspired the design of Alejandro's own boutique in New York. 'The walls are adorned with nostalgic black and white images of my grandfather's factory and store, and mid-century furniture is mixed with modern lighting and fixtures, bringing the past together with the new.'

Whether it's down to the business acumen that runs in his family or his own outgoing, creative, detail-oriented and driven personality, Alejandro has embraced the rite of passage with great success. He has been among the CFDA/*Vogue* Fashion Fund top ten candidates, and has twice been nominated for the Swarovski Award for Accessory Design.

On one memorable night at New York's leading Latino cultural institution, 'I was presented with the Artistic Achievement Award at the 2014 El Museo del Barrio gala.'

Of his shoe-designing process, Alejandro notes that at the very start he studies the shape he wants to achieve, looking closely at how it will fit the form of the foot. 'Creating a shoe is like a puzzle. Only once this is resolved do I start thinking about materials, colours, and so on. For the rest of the process, I go through different stages of sampling until we get to the final prototype.' As he notes, 'You need to lay down a strong foundation for shoes just like you do for a house.'

Working in his atelier, which is directly above his store, enables him to be close to his customers and to experience their feedback first-hand. 'I'm always moved by the utter love that people have for shoes, and especially the emotional response that people have when they wear my shoes,' he smiles. These are hand-stitched, and that makes them part of an exclusive club with only a few other up-scale brands. The prices, of course, reflect the degree of quality and craftsmanship involved, and sometimes Alejandro regrets 'the lack of knowledge and appreciation of how complicated it is to make high-end shoes'. He does not dwell too much on it, however, as he is always focusing on what his next project might be.

When prompted to think of an alternative career he could have had, he comes up with a surprising answer: 'Honestly? Probably a farmer. I love the idea of planting seeds, growing crops and working the land.' Actually it's not so surprising, since Alejandro's primary love is for the act of making with his own hands. Like tending the land, designing shoes requires devotion, patience and a certain gift that only a few are lucky enough to have.

*www.alejandroingelmo.com*

'My muse is a vision of a truly modern woman who is independent, sexy and glamorous. I think about what she should be wearing when she's going out. The sidewalk is her red carpet, so I want her to look major at all times!'

*(opposite)* A fourth-generation shoemaker, Alejandro Ingelmo can trace his family history through black and white photographs of his great-grandfather's factory and staff in Cuba.

*(right)* 'Culebra' stiletto-heeled sandal in calfskin, with gold *specchio* (mirror) accents.

*(clockwise from top left)* 'Boomerang' pointed-toe stiletto-heeled pump in bronze *specchio* (mirror) calfskin; 'Cece' platform wedge in black pony-style calfskin, with faux lace-up and buckle details; 'Mariposa' peep-toe stiletto-heeled bootie, with black suede upper and silver Swarovski crystal panels; 'Via Flat' criss-cross multi-strap flat ankle sandal in silver *specchio* leather; 'Mariposa' stiletto-heeled pump-style bootie in fuchsia suede and nubuck; 'Tron' sneaker in black glove leather, with gold-tone cut-out side panels and signature toecap insets.

(top) 'Mariposa' peep-toe stiletto-heeled
bootie in metallic silver calfskin;
(above) 'Mariposa' pump-style stiletto-
heeled bootie in black calfskin.

*(above)* **Campaign image [replicated] for the 'Tron' sneaker in silver iridescent cotton canvas, with high-gloss cut-out side panels and toecap insets.**

*(above left)* 'Odyssey Iridescent' peep-toe stiletto-heeled cage bootie in calfskin, with turquoise stamped iridescent leather insets; *(above right)* 'Flavia' pointed-toe stiletto-heeled d'Orsay pump in turquoise stamped iridescent leather, with black patent leather side strap.

ALEKSANDER

SIRADEKIAN

When a designer's first collection is named 'Megalomania', one immediately gets a hint of a self-deprecating sense of humour and the fact that anything its creator does may have to be taken with a pinch of salt. An amusing comic strip posted on his website shows a line-up of the most powerful trendsetters and public figures on the planet, all raving about and craving his glamorous shoes. Lo and behold, the fantasy is already coming to life. Fashion icons from Aleksander Siradekian's side of the world, namely Russia (magazine editors Victoria Davydova and Elena Peneva, fashion writers Evelina Khromtchenko and Daria Veledeeva), glossy magazines (*Vogue*, *Grazia*, *ELLE*) and online resources (Trendspace.ru) have all lined up behind the young prodigy. It will not take long before the rest of the world follows suit. After all, the name 'Megalomania' also conjures up the couture-style grandeur of his covetable shoes.

'I've been drawing and painting a lot since early childhood. I often took drawing lessons, and it seemed to me that the two hours of the lesson just flew by too fast,' Aleksander recalls. 'Later, I studied at the Tbilisi Academy of Arts, but sadly the war erupted in Georgia, so we had to move to Russia, where I now live and work. Against all odds, this upheaval did not stop me from pursuing my passion for art.'

The decision to venture into shoe design stemmed from a prominent influence throughout Aleksander's life: his grandmother. She was a shop superintendent at a chocolate factory in Tbilisi and Aleksander's principal recollection is of her 'slipping her snow-white starched overall over her dress before entering the shop and starting to give instructions to the employees. What a splendid silhouette, with her uniform completed by eight-centimetre [3 in.] high heels … unusually high for those times!' Aleksander's grandmother had a large collection of pumps in different colours, although it was very hard to acquire the Italian or Austrian shoes that were the pinnacle of fashion at the time.

'My grandmother was a regular customer of the best shoe workshops in Tbilisi,' Aleksander recounts. 'The first time I accompanied her and my mother to one, I immediately wanted to improve their order, as I was already a highly creative child. Understandably the owner wasn't thrilled, convinced that my childish ideas were going to ruin the costly commission.' But his grandmother asked everyone to let Aleksander express his suggestions. 'The owner eventually caved in and took the order under my guidance. I was no more than six years old. I was very worried because I understood that the shoes might not turn out to be as beautiful as I'd planned, and then I would simply have spoiled them. Waiting was a time filled with mixed emotions, but fortunately the end result pleased everyone.' Only later did Aleksander realize that the workshop owner must have privately figured out how to implement the major elements of his ideas, but, 'being a child', he quips, 'it seemed to me that I should take all the credit!'

Aleksander continued to join his grandmother when she went to the shoe workshops, and he began to accompany her friends as well. As he grew older, he 'started thinking fearlessly of not only decorative elements, but also complete looks. I like classic materials and forms, but, thanks to modern technologies, we can nowadays transform a classic product into an absolutely up-to-date and new one.'

At the moment Aleksander is enjoying creating shoes, but only time will tell what comes next in his creative future. 'I never know what will carry me away tomorrow: it might be refrigerator-tuning or jewelry art,' he muses. He is something of a chameleon, his mind hardwired to buzz with ideas, while his ability to make do in any circumstance remains strong. 'I don't need to adapt to a place, and I don't have a study either. It's enough for me to have a piece of paper and a pencil, and I will simply adjust the place to make it comfortable enough for me to kick-start my creative process,' he notes.

While he cites his childhood traits as 'impudence, confidence and a sense of aspiration', he has now settled into 'diligence, belief and a certain egoism'. With two compact collections per year – approximately twenty styles each – he has quickly developed a strong imprint. His signature adornment of tassels, evoking the silky manes of stallions or the military epaulettes worn by tsars, is astutely placed throughout all his collections. Whether it appears at the back of a pair of stilettos to give some aristocratic elegance or across the front of a moccasin, the tassel cascade is the *coup de génie* that makes these shoes immediately identifiable. Luxurious materials – including fine suede, patent leather, velvet, silk and lace (Aleksander once deposited a 20-carat diamond in the inlay of an open-toe sandal for an important client from the Middle East) – confirm the high-octane sophistication of his line once and for all.

'My shoes suit anyone who is ready to try on my bold vision of beauty and comfort,' he declares. 'At the end of the day, my product is for a special occasion, and any future owner should know for sure that their life is in itself a special occasion. So my motto is: "Enjoy my shoes as you would enjoy your life!"'

*www.siradekian.com*

*'I am an "egoist". I control the process one hundred per cent. I try not to keep myself within limits; instead, I open up to the possibilities of implementing ideas into a product. That way I enjoy both the process and the result of everything I do.'*

*(opposite above)* 'Liza Lace' pointed-toe stiletto-heeled pumps in mustard suede covered in black lace with black silk tassels, on either side of 'Liza' pointed-toe stiletto-heeled pumps in mustard suede with matching silk tassels; *(opposite below)* 'Nanyo Lace' pointed-toe stiletto-heeled pumps in petrol blue suede covered in black lace with black silk tassels, on either side of 'Nanyo' pointed-toe stiletto-heeled pumps in petrol blue suede with matching silk tassels.

*(clockwise from top left)* 'Dolly' pointed-toe stiletto-heeled pumps in blue and beige patent leather, with row of bows; 'Aleksander' moccasins in black patent leather, with black silk tassels; 'Nora' pointed-toe stiletto-heeled pumps in beige patent leather, with contrast cut-out delineation in black patent leather; 'Fatia' pointed-toe stiletto-heeled pumps in icy blue patent leather, with buckled straps in pairs; 'Liza' pointed-toe stiletto-heeled pumps in black and beige patent leather, with back cut-out yokes and contrast add-on stripes; 'Goga' pointed-toe stiletto-heeled pumps in red suede, with back cut-out yokes.

# ALLAN BAUDOIN

Made-to-measure. There is a thrilling ring to it; the promise of joining a sort of private club of connoisseurs who share a demand for excellence, a need for unique objects made to mirror their most personal requirements. The individual who takes up the made-to-order trade must also have courage and faith in the ideal of uncompromising standards. Meet bootmaker Allan Baudoin. A friend once described him as having 'a restless nature, a willingness to be constantly challenged and to try things, unafraid to take risks, drawn to perfection, and unable to stand mediocrity'. All these qualities make him the perfect candidate to have launched a bespoke brand.

Surprisingly, Allan originally specialized in sciences. 'After studying maths in Paris, I did my undergraduate studies in computer science and IT at University College London. I then went on to study management for my masters at London Business School. It's not exactly the classic shoemaking apprenticeship,' he admits. He found himself on the track of many able students – 'following the path of scientific studies at select universities in order to land a competitive high-paying job'. In Allan's case, this meant working on business strategy for technology companies and in quantitative marketing. Despite working for some prestigious employers, after two disappointing years he decided to look for a more fulfilling career and to set up on his own.

The rigour and precision of his scientific training may have played a part in his ability to design the perfect-fit shoe, but his decision to switch paths was actually prompted by a chance encounter with a shoemaker. 'We immediately connected. Seeing that I had a good sense for both shoemaking and business, he introduced me to his friends, and I started to get to know the very small world of bespoke shoemakers. As I learned the craft and the trade, I started to meet more and more highly qualified artisans, and to build a network of uniquely skilled craftsmen and suppliers.' Allan designed his first shoes – 'the most beautiful pair of Chelsea boots I had ever seen' – and worked on the production line and supply chain. The interest his first designs generated made him realize that what he thought had been a personal quest actually addressed a gap in the market. The fact that the challenge was so enjoyable was a bonus.

'In my case,' Allan says, 'designing is a continuous process of creation, from a sketch or idea to a final product. As you are making every shoe by hand, you are still designing. It's that process that I'm passionate about. Every single shoe I make is unique and reflects my customers' needs and tastes. My role is to translate and integrate those into my creations. When I make shoes, I work as if the customer were in the room with me, inspecting every detail.'

Trying to pin down Allan's style is not easy. With a multicultural background – of French and Chinese-Panamanian origins, he grew up in Paris but has lived in London all of his adult life – he reckons his taste is closer to the French, 'but without being as traditional and conservative.

On the other hand my shoes are made in London and Northampton, and this also influences the designs. I would say that they find their aesthetic roots in France, but the craftsmanship is as English as can be. The "handmade in England" element is key for my shoes, but they are essentially European.'

With three 'base' designs already on offer – they form one collection and can be customised to make around twenty distinct 'styles' – Allan has five new bases in the pipeline. 'With made-to-measure, requests vary a lot, and so every shoe is a new design challenge. You have to re-think all the details every time, so that they come out looking perfect,' he notes. 'It's a very fine balance between a stunning shoe and an ordinary one. Everything is in the little details.' Classic yet modern, Allan's sleek, simple and elegant creations are utterly authentic, 'because I don't try to be different for the sake of it'. The 'difference' lies in his care and his expert touches. The consistent use of hand-dyeing on the finest calf leather – the most requested so far being dark green antiqued, which has 'small reflections and variations, just like the shell of a scarab', in contrast to the dull, uniform colours tanneries often supply – makes for a particularly refined and arresting look. Allan cuts the leather himself by hand on a cutting board. Eschewing the idea of fast fashion and plastics, chemicals and industrial products as much as possible, he notes, 'My home studio in East London is a bit like an alchemist's laboratory, with glass bottles filled with all kinds of colourful liquids.'

Ultimately he would like to change the way people look at men's versus women's footwear. 'I can't see why they are categorized as so distinct from one another. Women should be able to enjoy more of the comfort and quality associated with the best men's shoes, and in turn men's shoes could draw more inspiration from the creativity and experimentation of women's footwear,' he states. His shoes appeal widely to those who dare to experiment and who like to dress in a more masculine and enigmatic way. These customers flock to 'The Baby Shop', the nickname given by Allan's friends to the tiny space: 'a shoe-lover's mini-treasure chest, enveloping you in the smell of leather and the art of shoemaking'. Those lucky clients find that they have just stepped into shoe heaven.

*www.allanbaudoin.com*

*(clockwise from top left)* Hand-clicking (cutting) a vamp for a burgundy Oxford lace-up; shaping the curve of a leather heel block; using paper annotated with measurements to modify a made-to-measure last; 'The Carlin' Oxford lace-ups in dark brown calf suede, with toecap broguing and zigzag gimping.

*(opposite left)* 'The Hicks' Chelsea boots in black calf suede; *(opposite right)* 'The Pryor' double-buckle monkstraps in hand-dyed dark green antiqued calfskin.

'Despite the recent prevalence of fast fashion, there will always be people who marvel, as I do, at the beauty of craftsmanship, handed down from one generation of shoemakers to the next, carrying history and substance.'

(this page) 'The Carlin' Oxford lace-ups in dark brown calf suede, with toecap broguing and gimping; 'The Hicks' Chelsea boots in dark green antiqued calfskin; 'The Hicks' Chelsea boots in black calf suede.

(opposite) 'The Pryor' double-buckle monkstraps in grained burgundy calfskin.

# AMÉLIE PICHARD

Screen starlets meet California babes, the 1940s and 1980s collide, and old-time Americana takes on a subversive sex appeal. Each of Amélie Pichard's campaigns combines femininity with a certain cinematic storytelling. Think Lana del Rey's music videos, but more polished. 'I could easily have been a rock star or, better, a glamour photographer,' says Amélie. 'When I was younger, I couldn't stop drawing gorgeous female silhouettes. Nothing else interested me.' That said, her shoes themselves paradoxically revolve around a tomboyish-tinged allure and cool sophistication. 'My design approach increasingly reflects my own personality: strong, playful and off-the-wall. My inspiration comes from directors like David Lynch, photographers like Guy Bourdin, an era I have not known (the 1960s and '70s), and a country I do not live in (the USA)!'

Regardless of the North American fantasy world that inspires Amélie so deeply, her shoes end up looking unquestionably French. They are extremely wearable, plus they have just the right touch of retro to make them utterly modern. According to Amélie, it is very Anglo-Saxon to devise quirky or very high-heeled shoes, whereas, as a busy Parisian woman herself, she designs shoes for 'working women who have to be presentable at all hours of the day. They cannot play dress-up when they show up at a supermarket on their way home at the end of their shift. My fundamental rule is to create shoes that allow you to walk in the street.' But, she notes, 'I'm not an artist, and therefore I have to be cautious how I translate my sometimes peculiar ideas into footwear.'

Crocodile skin would be her ultimate choice when it comes to material. However, since it is too expensive for her commercial positioning, she astutely opts for faux-crocodile instead, while alternating fierce finishes including metallic, matt, glossy and varnished. 'I also venture into more unconventional territory when it comes to materials: cork, tortoiseshell-printed leather and pink sheepskin, to name but a few,' she adds. As each new season approaches, she imagines new narratives that will dictate her choice of textures and shapes. The actual sketching is always kept until last, just prior to the final allocation of colours and components. 'Once the sketch and the first sample are out, it all happens very fast. It takes about one month to get the final item,' Amélie explains. 'Each season brings the opportunity for reinvention, and that's why I adore the blank-canvas stage. As a designer who primarily story-tells, I create 3D items instead of laying my tales out on paper.'

Amélie studied styling and model-making at Mod'Art in Paris. She then went on to head the ready-to-wear creative studio at the fashion company Dice Kayek for five years, where she says she learned all the skills necessary to manage a small business. 'Today I am a "master" at multitasking, juggling five to six trades at once,' she smiles. It was a meeting in 2008 with a certain Madame Germaine, the last shoemaker in Belleville, Paris, that was a catalyst in setting Amélie's shoemaking future in motion. She complemented her training with a six-month stint at Eric Lomain,

an orthopedic bootmaker – not your expected glamorous outpost, but it offered a valuable crash course in honing her craft.

On submitting her first ever solo collection, 'American Girl', to shoe retailer Bata's 'Jeunes Créateurs' competition in 2010, Amélie was rewarded with top prize, and just as importantly exposure, recognition and a huge boost in self-confidence. 'That was the first time I had designed shoes, and six months later I could see them on everyone's feet.' Since then, she has been lauded for her pioneering spirit and mature business branding, winning the 'Grand Prix de la Création de la Ville de Paris' and being selected among the new talents to look out for in the 'ELLE aime la mode' competition, run by French ELLE magazine.

This vanguard designer confides that she works best under pressure, but she also thrives 'on planes, with no phone or Web connection'. She takes pleasure in bonding with her customers, who often become friends. She is also good at strategic planning, recognizing the need for a second line with a focus on eco-credentials and animal-free production. 'The future is in sustainable fashion,' she states. 'It's in creating with a conscience. The challenge I've set myself is to render vegan products sexy and desirable.'

Like many pragmatic designers, Amélie is not concerned with reinventing the wheel, but rather with updating it using the tools that progress continues to make available. 'I use the widely shared method of welding – different adhesives joining the upper and the sole of the shoe. Nothing special there: this is a very traditional shoemaking technique, and I like it precisely for that reason.'

Having said that, Amélie's credo is 'working "classic" shoe templates with new techniques, and using never-before-seen juxtapositions of components'. She likes to keep in mind what Coco Chanel once said: 'La mode se démode, le style jamais (Fashion goes out of fashion, style never does). This is still highly relevant.' So when an existing customer owns fifteen pairs of Amélie Pichard shoes and counting, it certainly augurs well that this is one designer who is poised to stand the test of time … in style.

*www.ameliepichard.com*

*(this page)* A modern sexy/glam chic vibe permeates Amélie Pichard's Parisian studio, thanks to objects and moodboards that reinforce the creative ethos of the house.

*(opposite)* Campaign image [replicated] of 'Chloé' booties in pink perforated velvet and patent leather, with raw heel.

*'My shoes are slightly unorthodox yet wearable; sexy but casual; vintage but unmistakably urban.'*

*(opposite above)* 'Candy' pointed-toe pumps in khaki Lurex and velvet; *(opposite below)* 'Candy' pointed-toe pumps in silver Lurex and dusty pink velvet, worn with matching 'Abag' bag in velvet with crocodile jewel.

*(this page, clockwise from left)* 'Nancy' ankle boots in green velvet and Lurex; 'Candy Socks' pumps in green velvet, with integrated Lurex socks; 'Coco' Oxford lace-ups in full blue velvet.

*(top row, left to right)* 'Guy' platform slide in pink patent leather; 'Coco' brogue in navy perforated velvet; 'Jeanne' mule in black crackled lambskin; *(centre)* 'Charlotte' ankle-strap sandal in white crackled lambskin; 'Colette' wedged brogue in brown glazed leather; 'Chloé' boot in pink perforated velvet and patent leather, with raw heel; *(bottom)* 'Coco' brogue in pink sheepskin; 'Abag' bag in black crackled lambskin with gold crocodile jewel.

*(opposite)* Campaign image [mirrored] of 'Jeanne' mules in navy patent leather.

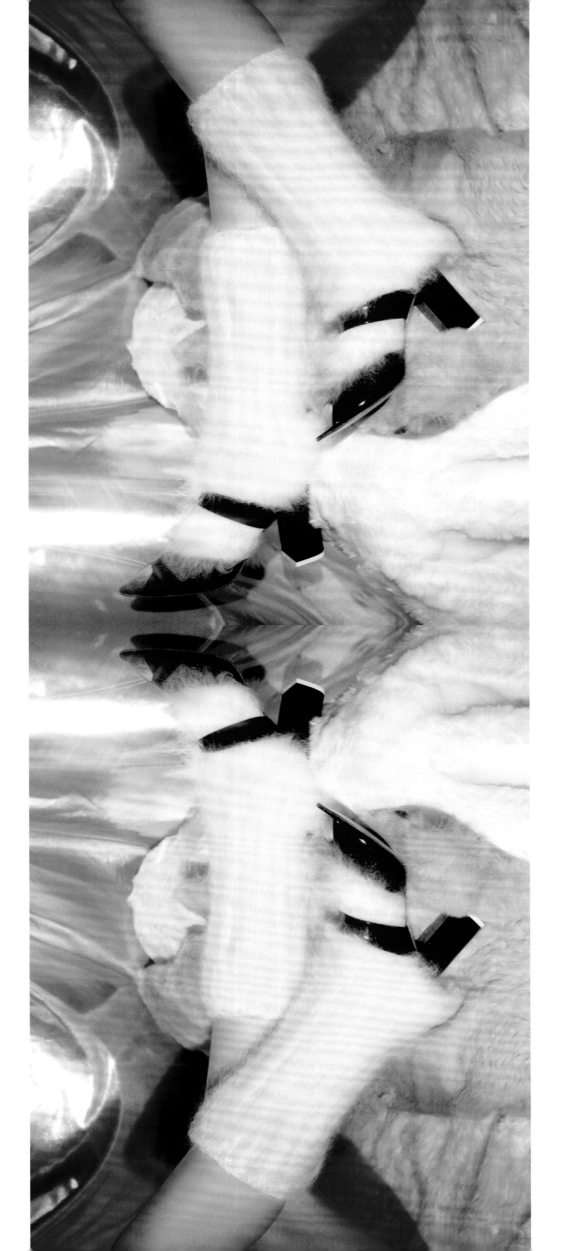

ANDREIA CHAVES

Brazilian designer Andreia Chaves envisions innovative shoes that pay as much homage to futuristic architecture as they do to exclusive craftsmanship. Her avant-garde luxury concept combines industrial design with handmade processes, producing shoes that are like nothing we have seen before, but that continue to offer elegance and functionality. In her 'Goldsculpt' and 'Outline' series, a masterful torsion of lines softens the edges so that each shoe, rather than looking excessively sharp, becomes a feat of feminine construction. A sense of movement is also delivered, as golden straps twirl like metal in fusion or patent leather ribbons wrap the foot in a warm embrace. Empty spaces are as important as solid components.

This approach to design and question of balance is inherent in all Andreia's creations. 'I would say I'm a designer and architect,' she affirms. 'Designing shoes or clothes means working around the human body, respecting its anatomy and natural movement, and at the same time creating a relationship with the space around it. It's similar to architecture, though on a much smaller scale.' Indeed, her bold designs also resemble shoe-size sculptures, boasting both rigour and fluidity. But, like the best structures, they are as comfortable to inhabit as they are beautiful to behold.

Her earlier creations, such as the 'InvisibleShoe' collection, were more conceptual in essence. 'Today,' Andreia states, 'I try to strike a balance between articulating my own language and keeping the product marketable.' Her cutting-edge experimentations have put her on the map of the most ingenious shoe designers of our time.

Some of her models bear a resemblance to armour; fashionable shields for design-driven women. With the 'InvisibleShoe' series, the foot might be encased in a faceted carapace (the version made of laser-cut acrylic mirrored façades, looking like something from outer space fiction) or else housed within a geodesic hub (the version with a laser-cut nylon black shell). 'People usually say my work is "fresh",' admits Andreia, 'which I consider to be a real compliment. For me, the future will keep bringing new materials and technologies that will change the way designers conceive and develop ideas.'

Andreia is also a firm believer in craftsmanship. 'I think people are looking at this more and more when they buy new products. Craft is the trend for the future.' All her shoes are handmade by skilled artisans in Italy, and she does her utmost to source the finest components. 'Since the beginning of my career I've enjoyed exploring different materials for my designs. Leather is without doubt the most used material for shoes, so it's inevitable that it's considered for at least part of the composition. I now associate it with wood for the heels.'

Andreia does not regard illustration as one of her strengths, so she avoids designing in 2D. 'Going through a 3D model is always much more exciting, and it makes you understand all the possibilities or flaws in a design,' she observes. This explains why brainstorming around a prototype is such a pivotal moment in her design process. She believes in experimenting to the fullest with the concept she has in mind, so as not to leave it to chance for any shoe idea to be the most realized it can be. On a more pragmatic note, the prototype also of course helps Andreia to understand the potential and feasibility of her project.

Her original interest in design was not particularly focused on shoes. 'I started watching people on the street. Then I began to notice the shoes they were wearing. Consequently I started looking at what was available in the stores and I began to buy books on shoe design. It was only when I started designing my own styles that I realized this was something I should probably study further,' she recounts. She studied multimedia design at Senac São Paulo, then footwear and accessories design at the prestigious Polimoda Fashion Institute in Florence. Not long after graduating, she took the world of contemporary fashion by storm with her 'InvisibleShoe'. Nowadays Andreia is a sought-after design consultant, splitting her time between Europe and Brazil, all the while steadily growing her own shoe line.

Distinctive designs, of course, call for a distinctive approach. Trends and the international fashion calendar are foreign notions to Andreia. 'My launches are irregular and absolutely not seasonal.' Marching to the beat of one's own drum is essential for any visionary, but it has an extra advantage when it comes to fashion: it makes those creations exclusive and unique in a market saturated with mass-offerings. 'I am so happy to be able to work with limited editions and thereby support local Italian artisans,' says Andreia. 'When it comes to the whole fashion industry, I don't like the fact that people can consume without even considering exactly what they're buying, in terms of what the materials are, what conditions the object has been produced in, and so on.'

We can only wait in eager anticipation for what new technologies, such as 3D printing, might inspire in such a determined designer. Series after series Andreia rides the crest of the pioneering wave, all the while bringing design and fashion ever closer together.

*www.andreiachaves.com*

*(this page)* Highly skilled artisans cutting the leather for a shoe pattern; sewing the upper; and assessing the measurements while assembling a shoe.

*(opposite above left)* 'Goldsculpt Couture Shoe: Style Three' in beige lambskin, with highly polished bronze and 24K-gold-plated structure; *(opposite above right)* 'Goldsculpt Couture Shoe: Style Two' in navy blue lambskin, with 24K-gold-plated structure; *(opposite below)* 'Goldsculpt Couture Shoe: Style One' in black goat nappa leather, with 24K-gold-plated structure.

*(this page)* '**Outline**' sandals in leather, with sculptural wooden heels.

*'I am very excited by the possibility of creating designs that are different from anything that is on the market today.'*

(top) 'InvisibleShoe' with external 3D printed nylon structure, laser-cut mirrored façades and leather on the inside; (above) 'Invisible NakedVersion' with external 3D printed nylon structure and internal leather.

APERLAï

It took only four years for Aperlaï, the trailblazing French shoe company founded by Alessandra Lanvin, to have the red carpet rolled out for it at the Footwear News Summit held in New York City in 2012. 'Aperlaï was invited as keynote speaker, as it was considered "one of the industry's most dynamic players and fastest rising stars"', enthuses Alessandra. To talk of a meteoric ascent is an understatement. Moreover the brand has not lost any momentum in establishing itself as a front-runner. Over its few years of existence, Aperlaï has already been selected to be part of several major exhibitions, including 'Killer Heels: The Art of the High-Heeled Shoe' at Brooklyn Museum, for which two iconic Aperlaï styles were chosen, and 'Shoe Obsession' at the museum of New York's Fashion Institute of Technology, which also includes Aperlaï in its permanent collection. From new kid on the block to fashion-reference status in no time, and all thanks to Alessandra's innate fascination for creating beautiful, nothing-quite-like-it footwear.

'I've always been fascinated by shoes and accessories,' she declares. 'I used to cherish the moments spent at the Massaro atelier in Paris, where my mother would order her shoes. For as long as I can remember, I've been collecting shoes myself – special editions or unique pieces. They're like a display of sculptures in my wardrobe!' It was when she was pregnant with her son that she realized she should create her own shoe line. 'I realized that the majority of women's shoe designers were, in fact, men. So I thought that creating from a woman's perspective could make a difference.'

Alessandra had already worked for several years as a headhunter in the fashion retail and luxury goods industry. She was therefore in a good position to refine her vision of both the high-end market and Italian craftsmanship prior to embarking on her solo career. 'To be a headhunter requires you to find the right qualities and skills in people to fill strategic positions. In that sense I think the most important thing I developed during those years was an eye for picking the right network of suppliers and collaborators.'

Paris is the city where Alessandra primarily finds her inspiration, having her studio on rue du Bac in the elegant 7th arrondissement. However, it is in Italy that her shoes come to life, thanks to the efforts of the finest craftsmen. 'A strong network of artisans and suppliers, all based in Italy, are involved in the shoes' creation. This gives them a significant and specialized added value,' stresses Alessandra.

Had she not ventured into the shoe industry, she says she would probably have turned to contemporary art, especially painting. It seems safe to suggest that she has, in fact, merged the two successfully in Aperlaï as it stands today. She repeatedly credits the same illustrious list of artists – Jackson Pollock, Picasso, Mondrian, Ettore Sottsass – as sources from whom she takes her creative cues. These founts of inspiration are evident in Aperlaï's modernist, structural forms combined with effective colour-blocking and a component-focused simplicity. Alessandra's feat resides in the subtle feminization of references that are otherwise markedly 'no-frill'.

She accomplishes this through a number of strategies, including the use of fine details to counterbalance solid elements, the employment of prints to give dimensionality, and the juxtaposition of precious skins alongside technical materials such as vinyl, Plexiglas and plastic.

Aperlaï's iconic signature is the graphic Geisha high heel. 'The 14-centimetre [5½ in.] heel is an ode to Cubism, inspired by Japanese tradition and elegance. It's finely realized in Florence and very light because it's made in thermoplastic ABS.' With Aperlaï shoes, dualities – solid versus delicate, geometric versus refined – are calibrated to succeed: coloured yokes delineate the outlines of shoes and thereby reinforce sensuality; bright furry pompoms punctuate super-sleek suede silhouettes (when added to python, the contrast works wonders in bringing complete modernity; one can scarcely imagine a snake and a mink co-existing outside Aperlaï's world); while the use of notches, whether in heels or the body of the shoes, resonates not with mechanics but rather with delicacy. As Alessandra points out: 'Details always matter.'

This attention to all factors comes together to inform a very strong visual identity that lends itself well to collaborations with individuals who delight in image-making, whether photographers (Martin Baebler, Olivier Marcillac, Alessandro Clemenza) or artists (the duo La Fratrie, the visual artist Marie Laffont). A cornerstone in Aperlaï's history arrived in 2014 with the opening of the company's first flagship store in Paris, complementing an already strong retail presence in the best boutiques across the globe.

'I'm a huge fan of Winston Churchill,' asserts Alessandra. '"We make a living by what we get, but we make a life by what we give."' This philosophy surely accompanies the creation of every Aperlaï shoe. And, as Alessandra says, 'A good design is a creation that survives time.' We can only envisage the brightest of futures for this ambitious game-changer.

*www.aperlai.com*

'I wanted to create a graphic signature: shoes with pure lines and a strong design, yet feminine.'

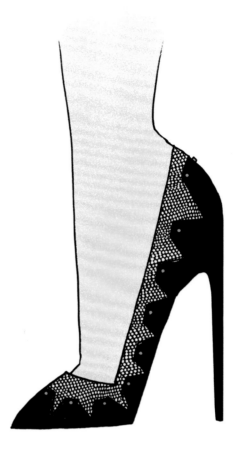

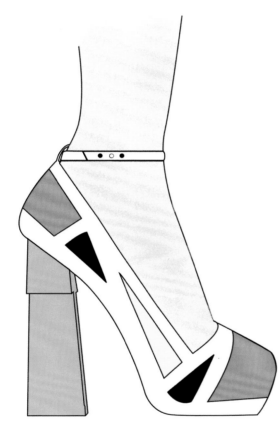

(opposite) A glimpse of Alessandra Lanvin's moodboard for her Fall/Winter 2014–15 collection.

(this page) Sketches for a 'Geisha Lines' sandal in pink, a 'Mecano' pump in black and a 'Cross Bootie' in crimson.

(opposite) 'High Simple B' high-heeled
pull-on knee boots in black suede and
custom petrol blue croc-effect leather.

(this page, top) 'Maelle' high-heeled
ankle-strap sandals in red snakeskin, with
matching suede fringes; (above) 'BonBon I'
high-heeled ankle-strap pumps in pink
woven textile and leather.

*(left column, top to bottom)* 'Mecano' high-heeled ankle boot in leather; 'Alana' slingback pump in colour-block woven textile, with razor-edge 'Zottsass' PVC heel; 'Memphis' high-heeled mule in snakeskin and leather; *(centre)* 'Pompom' internal-platform pump in leather, with black mink pompom and 'Geisha' heel; 'Gatsby' ballerina in suede, with mink pompom and leather trim; 'Pompom' high-heeled open-toe pump in suede, with pink mink pompoms; *(right)* 'Mercury Zottsass' high-heeled slingback sandal in suede, with razor-edge 'Zottsass' PVC high heel and island platform; 'Pico Hands' high-heeled open-toe sandal in leather, with rubber details; 'Agata Blue Klein' high-heeled slingback peep-toe sandal in calfskin.

*(opposite above left)* 'Geisha Doll' square-toe ankle-strap pumps in suede, with 'Geisha' heel; *(opposite above right)* 'Mercury Zottsass' high-heeled slingback sandals in woven textile and leather, with razor-edge 'Zottsass' PVC high heel and island platform; *(opposite below left)* 'Straps' high-heeled lace-up sandals in snakeskin and leather; *(opposite below right)* 'Memphis' high-heeled mules in green snakeskin and leather.

# AQUAZZURA

'Oscar de la Renta once said, "You should walk as if you have three men behind you." When you wear my shoes, you should have *five* men following you!' exults Edgardo Osorio. As founder of Aquazzura, a brand that has in its short existence garnered adulation from customers and magazine editors alike, Edgardo is the emissary of a *dolce vita* Latin sophistication and sensuality, coupled with American ease. 'I'm extremely proud and humbled that, in just three years, Aquazzura has become an international brand, selling in over 45 countries and garnering kudos from the press and buyers. The shoes sell out very quickly, so there are even waiting lists for some of the styles.' Among many highlights: 'I was very proud when the shoes from my collaboration with Olivia Palermo sold out in less than 24 hours on Net-A-Porter.'

Born in Cartagena, Colombia, Edgardo was raised between the hotspots of Barranquilla, Miami and London. 'When I look way back, I remember deciding to be a plastic surgeon,' he recalls. 'I never thought my parents would allow me to work in fashion, so I thought of becoming the most creative kind of doctor. Now it seems I make women beautiful, but in a much less drastic way!' Indeed, Aquazzura's aesthetics rest on a refined elegance that only a kind of surgical eye could achieve.

'Designing shoes comes to me naturally, like talking or breathing,' Edgardo asserts. 'At the age of fourteen, when I started interning in fashion design, I was already designing shoes one week into the job. My parents turned out to be incredibly supportive. I recall my father telling me, "Do whatever you want to do, but do it with love and be the best."'

Edgardo studied shoe and accessory design at the London College of Fashion, but for over a decade now has lived in Florence. Before setting up on his own he worked for several high-profile Italian brands, including Salvatore Ferragamo, Roberto Cavalli and René Caovilla, accumulating valuable experience and fine-tuning his 'luxury fashion' smarts. 'All the houses taught me so much about quality, fit and sublime craftsmanship.'

His own shoes are 'made in Italy', and more specifically in Tuscany. 'Most of my raw materials also come from the area, so we have greater control of quality.' It can take up to eight months from initial sketch to approval for production. 'It needs to be perfect. There's no point in making a pair of shoes that look great in your closet, but not nice on your feet. Moreover if a shoe hurts you won't be sexy, no matter how sexy the shoe is. I love to see girls be able to walk all day and dance all night in my shoes.'

Each season Edgardo is inspired by his muses: 'in the manner of Truman Capote's swans of the 1960s, the modern swans of today – Carine Roitfeld, Lauren Santo Domingo, Olivia Palermo, Sarah Rutson, India Hicks, Nati Abascal and Princess Deena Abdulaziz'. In addition, 'the two people who are always on my moodboards are Kate Moss and Giovanna Battaglia: they both represent the sort of sensuality, easy elegance and cool that I love'.

Edgardo grew up surrounded by women and, by his own admission, this has made him 'very much a ladies' man'. As he notes, 'I'm constantly feeding off the needs and wants of my girlfriends from around the world. I want them to feel and look amazing whenever they wear my shoes. It's truly about creating objects of desire.'

As for his creative space, nothing less than the extraordinary would suit this contemporary aesthete. Lo and behold, his offices are located in the Palazzo Corsini, a 16th-century palace on the River Arno, next to the Ponte Vecchio. 'The rooms where my shop and atelier are used to be the old Medici apartments. We still have the original frescoes. Florence was the birthplace of the Renaissance and modern fashion, so for me it's a place with creative magic in the air.' Paradoxically, Edgardo confides that he rarely designs in his office, preferring to be near the sea. 'I go and work in the south of Tuscany, or somewhere sunny in front of the beach, and design the entire collection over a weekend,' he reports.

Four collections a year, each with an average of seventy styles, plus two to three capsule collections or special projects, are designed to feed the appetites of Aquazzura's die-hard fans. Signature elements include the use of Yves Klein blue, strappy lace-up shoes, snakeskin and second-skin suede shoes ('suede shoes colour so beautifully,' notes the designer). 'The most unusual shoe I have done is the "Piña Colada". It has a handwoven and patchworked leather pineapple at the back of the heel. It instantly became iconic and has been one of my most photographed shoes ever.' Experimentation with luxury codes is a given. 'I developed a special kind of cashmere suede from my first season that is soft and perfect for my unlined shoes, such as "Sexy Thing".'

The editor-in-chief of a very important American magazine visited his showroom in Paris and tried on a pair of the 'Sexy Thing' model. 'She loved them so much that she left with them on her feet, and she kept wearing them every day during Fashion Week,' recalls Edgardo. 'She said they were like a caress to her feet and the most comfortable and sexy high heels she had ever worn.' An observation that aptly sums up the essence of Aquazzura.

*www.aquazzura.com*

**Sketches by Edgardo Osorio for Aquazzura:** *(from top)* 'French Lover' high-heeled lace-up bootie; 'Marahari' bejewelled high-heeled sandal; 'The Queen' bejewelled high-heeled sandal.

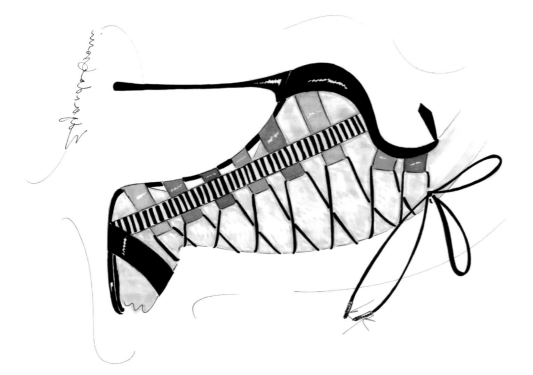

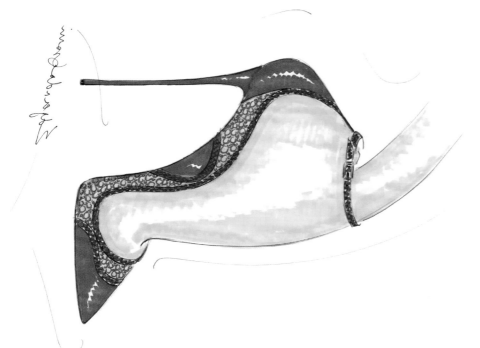

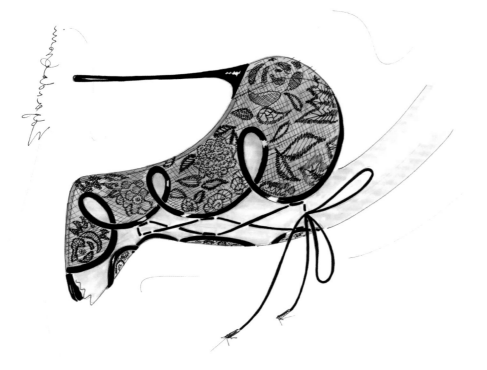

*(from top)* 'Beverly Hills Pop Art' high-heeled lace-up sandal; 'Memphis' high-heeled pointy pump; 'French Kiss' high-heeled lace-up bootie, with lace.

'I try to strike a balance between modern design, comfort and beauty, with a predilection for high heels. They give your body an amazing silhouette. They really put you on a pedestal.'

(above) 'French Lover' high-heeled lace-up open-toe booties in tonal grey snakeskin, with mesh details.

(opposite above) 'Positano' high-heeled pointy pump in multicoloured snakeskin and PVC; (opposite below) 'Jupiter' lace-up high-heeled open-toe bootie in yellow snakeskin, with cut-outs.

*(above)* 'Follow Me' high-heeled open-toe cage bootie in dark rose suede.

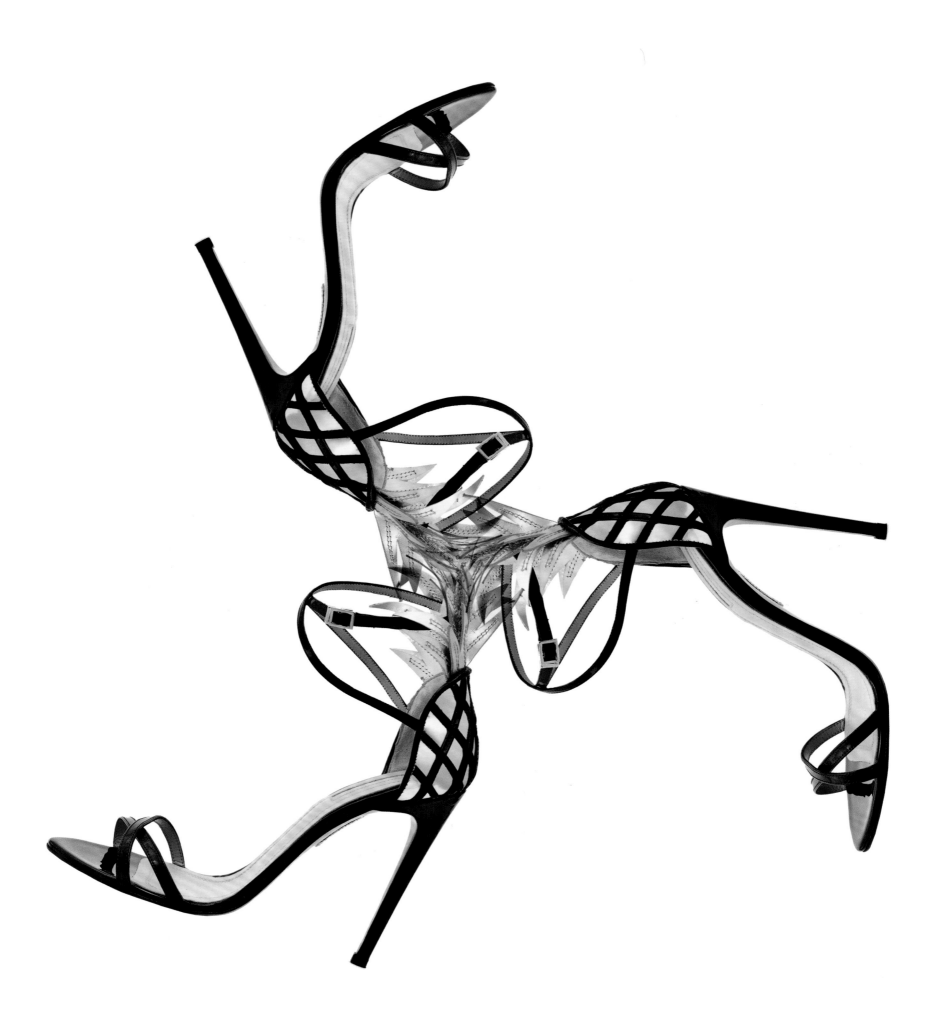

(above) 'Piña Colada' high-heeled strappy
sandal in black and gold patent leather,
with feathered pineapple-motif back.

*(top row, left to right)* 'Madison' high-heeled tie-up pump in black satin, with feather details and bow; 'Lola' high-heeled lace-up peep-toe sandal in black calfskin, with cut-outs; *(centre)* 'Eagle' high-heeled peep-toe bootie in black lace and suede; 'Belgravia' high-heeled lace-up pointy pump in forest green suede; 'Athena' high-heeled gladiator sandal in black calfskin; *(bottom)* 'Eagle' high-heeled pointy pump in black lace and suede.

*(top row, left to right)* 'Tie Me Up' high-heeled tie-up sandal in emerald satin; 'Charlotte' high-heeled tie-up peep-toe sandal in fuchsia satin; *(centre)* 'Beverly Hills' high-heeled lace-up bootie in red satin; 'Sexy Thing' high-heeled unlined bootie in dark rose suede, with cut-outs and back tie; 'Xena' high-heeled gladiator sandal in Blue Klein snakeskin, with multi-strand knotted straps; *(bottom)* 'Venus' high-heeled gladiator peep-toe bootie in black calfskin, with braiding details.

BRUNO
BORDESE

Welcome to an avant-garde streetwear scene; a luxury universe peopled with urban warriors, inner rock chicks and suave bikers. Blade Runner meets Studio 54. This is 'radical chic', according to Italian shoe designer Bruno Bordese … and, we may add, he shows it at its very best. 'I observe and design the future,' says Bruno. 'In the last twenty years globalization has deprived the world of individuality. However, young people today tend to prefer what is new, and as a result we're in a world where creativity is thankfully rewarded. My own designs are both easy and intellectual. The continuous study of forms and mixing of materials is part of my DNA. Day after day I try to improve what was created the day before.'

As far back as he can remember, Bruno has always wanted to be part of fashion hype and the art community; shoe designing was simply a logical direction. 'Even as a child, I was attracted to fashion, music, trends, shows… Back then I used to watch the reports about the New York clubs and I already felt I was part of that world,' he recalls. 'It was in the early 1980s – when the fashion system wasn't the same as it is today – that I went straight into working in a footwear showroom, right after I finished my school years. It didn't surprise my parents one bit. They also knew this was my calling.' Bruno confides that it has never felt like a job, but is, rather, an all-consuming passion that has led him to scrutinize every moment of the evolution of fashion and trends.

If he weren't a shoe wizard, he says he would probably have become an architect, a clothes designer or a DJ. These alternatives are not too far from what he has actually been doing all these years. 'I've been developing clear shapes, sporty chic lines, used effects and military-inspired looks. I'm an artist on one hand, an architect on the other. I feel close to the definition of "an artist who designs shoes by using the techniques of an architect".' He also notes that the shape of a shoe is key: 'It's exactly like the silhouette of a dress.' Since 1995 he has quietly been transforming the shoe industry by paring things back, by emancipating sportswear and giving it fashion status, and by putting revolutionary leather treatments under the spotlight.

'Ten years ago I made a pair of shoes, and I put them into a washing machine. This created the used effect that has been my signature ever since,' he explains. 'I treat my leathers with special washings until they look used, and so I obtain "imperfect" shoes with unusual looks, each one different from the next.' Touch, he says, is one of his most reliable senses. 'I just need to feel the leathers to understand the kind of manufacturing I can get from them.' This is very Italian in essence: culture, art, craftsmanship and fashion all rolled into one.

Bruno's résumé and self-description ('I'm a bit like Richard Gere in *American Gigolo*') attest to his preference for the more unconventional end of the luxury shoe spectrum. After ten years at Cesare Paciotti and another five with Alberto Guardiani, he eventually veered towards edgier houses such as Vivienne Westwood, Yohji Yamamoto, a.testoni, Casadei, Roberto Cavalli and Rochas Paris, before creating his own brand. 'I'm passionate about seeing people wearing my shoes; the way in which they always personalize and interpret them differently.'

Of his design process, he notes, 'Each idea becomes reality, like a unique piece of art.' It all starts from the trend of the season, which morphs into an idea that he then transfers into a drawing. 'Then I focus on the choice of materials and shapes, and from there we develop the design and it's perfected until you obtain the finished product. In all honesty, you can never stop perfecting.'

Over the years Bruno has used many varied materials, from python to toad to ostrich, but today hand-processed nappa and soft leathers are crucial to him. With about twenty collections a year – in other words, a whopping thousand unique styles – Bruno finds that the best time for brainstorming is at night. 'Often I work during the night because it's relaxing and I can concentrate. When the town sleeps, I am awake. I put on some music, and then I instinctively draw,' he states.

His creations are like armour, both voluminous and protective (fur, buckles, studs, spikes), which in turn makes them empowering. It is as if he has anticipated the mean streets out there and wants to equip his clients to confront urban chaos in style. In essence, his approach is about confidence and timeless allure. His collections are beautifully crafted for the realities of everyday life, so that you can pound the tarmac, run from point A to B, and party the night away, all while feeling supremely sexy. It was some fifteen years ago, in Japan, that Bruno was first called a 'maestro'. Well, time surely flies, but some things never change.

*www.brunobordese.com*

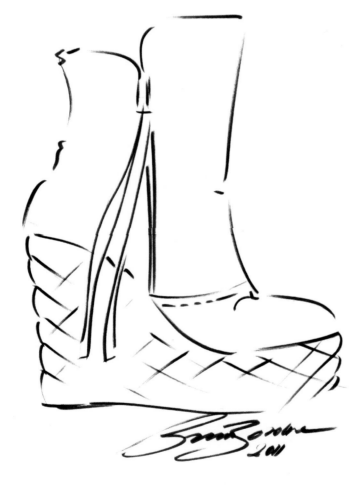

'My signature colours are white, which is a symbol of purity, and black, which is a must for elegance; and the technique that has always characterized my shoes is leather washing.'

*(this page)* **Bruno's vivacious sketches, which make his hand-drawn designs look like silhouettes on the move.**

*(opposite, clockwise from top left)* **Platform peep-toe bootie entirely covered in woven raffia; platform peep-toe bootie entirely covered in woven optical black and white checkerboard leather, with zip on back; wedge slingback sandal in black and white boa-printed leather; brogue in black and white Pollock-printed leather.**

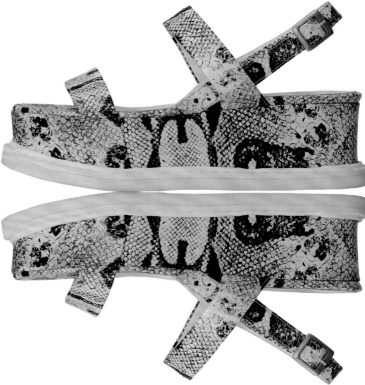

*(this page, clockwise from top left)* **Punk-inspired (King's Road, London, early 1980s) platform high boot in absolute black shiny nappa leather, with antique silver buckles; high sneaker in black suede, with Swarovski details and lateral zip; wooden wedge slingback sandal in black leather, with rubber sole.**

*(opposite, clockwise from top left)* **Wooden wedge sandal in black suede, with multiple silver buckles; raffia wedge sandal in black nappa leather, with multiple buckles; woven raffia wedge slingback sandal, with rubber sole.**

*(opposite)* High sneakers in white nappa leather, with studs and lateral zip; wooden wedge slingback sandal in black nappa leather, with rubber sole.

*(this page)* Wedge slingback sandal in black braided leather; wedge peep-toe bootie in black braided leather; low-rise peep-toe wedge bootie in black neoprene with orange rubber-coated elastic stripes and rubber sole.

BURAK
URYAN

Greatness can come out of turmoil. Shoe designer extraordinaire Burak Uyan best composes his architecturally driven shoes when surrounded by what he calls 'inspirational chaos'. 'All my boards of images, materials and colour cards are all over the place. Paired with some fun jams playing in the background, these are my preferred working conditions,' he smiles. Not just clutter, this panoply of paraphernalia attests to Burak's own ebullient spirit. As is the case with many artists, the ultimate work of art can easily emerge from an abundance of ideas and references.

In Burak's case, he creates shoes that brim with visual appeal, but also promise sensory and emotive experience. 'I once had an architecture masters graduate on my staff, and I really enjoyed her perspective. She described my creative style as an "aesthetic of sensation". She thought the pieces could be seen as devices of artistic expression that evoke sensations. It's not just the wearer that derives pleasure from the piece; it can elicit sensations in the spectator as well.'

Architecture is evidently Burak's main source of inspiration (he would love to collaborate with masters such as Santiago Calatrava and Bjarke Ingels, pairing their knowledge with his aesthetics), but he also taps eagerly into the art movements of Constructivism and Functionalism. 'Architectural construction elements can be applied to heels and details, while paintings and collages can become sources for textural development and colour inspiration. My creations end up being very sensual and feminine, yet they retain a graphic and bold quality. I see shoes as wearable pieces of art, so I try to engineer creations through provocative form and comfortable functionalism.'

Burak processes ideas from the worlds of art and design with great facility. 'I make sure to be aware of what is happening not only in fashion but also in other disciplines. I find an open mind is what keeps my designs intriguing and on their toes,' he notes. 'Right now I'm being influenced by kinetic art, figuring out ways of incorporating visual movement into my collection by taking basic shapes, transforming them through different techniques and instilling a futuristic feel into them. One must learn the rules in order to know which ones should be broken. I'm not a rebel without a cause, but I do like to provoke. What can be most challenging is to keep your mind and creations unconditioned: you always find a solution in the end.'

Burak makes the most of being a true cosmopolitan. German-born of Turkish heritage, he studied in Austria and has been living in Paris for over thirteen years. He revels in travel and getting a taste for different cultures, but the Bastille area where he works is in itself an inspirational environment: 'an artsy cultural melting pot', as he puts it. 'It enriches my mind and has influenced my designs toward contemporary pieces with an edge.' The spark of creative energy is often ignited by the allocation of materials to a particular style. 'Pairing contrasting colours, materials, patterns and prints – for example, a woven mix of snakeskin, metal threads and PVC – and watching the structure take on its own personality is a joy,' he says, 'and I love discovering original techniques and treatments.'

His silhouettes and proportions are always on point, even when featuring complex structures. Emerging from the sharp cuts and angles are designs that are sleek and composed. This effect is reinforced by the use of ultra-luxurious reptile skins such as water snake, karung, python and crocodile, all in various finishes, including printed, laminated and perforated.

Shoe designing has not always been Burak's speciality. He worked for many years as a womenswear designer for prestigious fashion houses such as Givenchy, and was the head designer at Giambattista Valli for five years. It was at the latter that he headed up his first shoe collection. 'That's when I developed a deep passion for shoes. It became like a drug,' he recalls. 'It was a real learning curve for me on the ground, working very closely with the artisans and technicians. Shoe designing is a completely different domain from ready-to-wear; it's more like haute couture, in a sense. It's all about mathematics and perfect proportions between last, platform and heel.'

During his time as a clothes designer Burak perceived that what excited women the most was shoes. 'There's nothing like watching a woman unpack a beautiful pair of shoes; the expression in her eyes when she tries them on,' he muses. Soon his shoemaking trajectory became unstoppable, as the fashion in-crowd began to take notice. At a ceremony in New York, attended by the legendary Manolo Blahnik, he was presented with the Vivian Infantino Emerging Talent Award, named in honour of the former fashion director of *Footwear News*, who had supported young talent throughout her career.

'In the early 1990s, designers used to consider shoes as just add-ons, only there to complete an outfit but without too much attention being paid to them. Nowadays, however, the position of shoes has changed drastically. They rule the look and give both identity and character to an outfit. They also reflect the personality of the woman who wears them.' So who is the archetypal Burak Uyan woman? 'She is sophisticated, confident and spontaneous, with a strong character. She teases the audience with her carefree attitude. So I always say: "Go for an extravagant pair!" They are my true works of art.'

*www.burakuyan.com*

'I would describe my work as a juxtaposition of contrasting materials, following organic and graphic lines, on sculptural heels.'

(this page) The birth of a shoe, via hand-sketching and looking at architectural and geometric patterns for inspiration.

(opposite, clockwise from top left) 'Bauhaus' sandal with graphic lines and cut-out elements on lacquered tubular heel and platform, shown in black and white lambskin and suede with black lambskin piping; salmon and white lambskin and suede with black lambskin piping; nude crocodile and lambskin with black lambskin piping; and pistachio crocodile and lambskin with black lambskin piping and silver metallic leather.

*(left column, from top to bottom)* **Lace-up boot** in black lizardskin, with black fox shield at front and wooden cone heel; ankle boot in ruby and navy lambskin, with light gold metal under wedge heel; sculpted-stiletto-heeled lace-up platform sandal with zigzag lines in black and white positive/negative-effect dot-printed water snake; sculpted-high-heeled ankle boot with triangle side cut-out and ankle strap in salvia buffalo leather, with lambskin interlacing detail at front; platform sandal with organic lines and ankle strap in saffron ponyskin and lambskin on lacquered tubular heel; *(centre)* ankle bootie with wave-line décolleté in black laser-cut ponyskin and black lambskin on high heel; ankle-strap sandal with V-shaped décolleté in rust suede and printed python on stiletto heel; high-heeled gladiator sandal with organic décolleté in black lambskin with light gold studs; high-heeled T-bar pump with triangular yokes in turquoise, royal blue and red suede, with black lambskin wrist and ankle straps; pump in olive crocodile, with light gold metal under wedge heel; *(right)* ankle-strap mid-heel cage-style Mary Jane in ruby lambskin and black and striped water snake; high-heeled T-bar pump with triangular yokes in olive and plum printed python, with plum lambskin wrist and ankle straps; peep-toe ankle boot with graphic cut-out elements in jade lambskin and water snake on stiletto heel.

 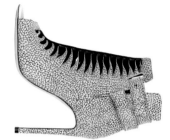 

*(left column, from top to bottom)* Ankle-strap island platform sandal with wrist strap in orange and pink suede and lambskin on lacquered tubular heel; peep-toe stiletto-heeled pump in pink and white marble-print silk satin and pink lambskin; high-heeled pump with cut-out details and drop-shaped wrist strap in lime, black and white lambskin with purple lizard inlays; *(centre)* belted peep-toe stiletto-heeled ankle boot with 'cut and twist' detail in printed nubuck and black lambskin; multi-strap sandal in royal blue water snake and lambskin on stiletto heel; asymmetric strappy sandal with triangular side elements in turquoise suede and purple lambskin on stiletto heel; strappy sandal with circle cut-outs and inlays in royal blue and red lambskin on stiletto heel; criss-cross ankle-strap sandal with overlapping front straps in red, purple and nude suede on stiletto heel; *(right)* strappy sandal with circle cut-outs and inlays in jade lambskin and water snake on stiletto heel; gladiator sandal in purple karung skin on architectural metal-constructed cylinder heel; stiletto-heeled slingback pump with wrist and ankle strap in light pale violet and mint lambskin and black and white striped water snake, with PVC inlay; lace-up bootie in red laser-cut lambskin on stiletto heel; flat sandal with large wristband in natural water snake, with tubular criss-cross ankle strap in white patent leather, front strap in silver metallic leather and yellow patent leather back.

CHARLINE

DE LUCCA

Is architecture gender-neutral? Some of us would probably define high-rises as masculine, with all their imposing, angular stature, but when Charline De Luca says her architectural shoes have become more feminine with time – 'I've tried to reconcile my architectural inspiration with my feminine side' – the outcome is empowering, yet sensual. Lines are sharp and concise, proportions are balanced, materials are sophisticated and edgy, and colours are mostly primary. In other words, these are shoes that merge a Guy Bourdin aesthetic with an I. M. Pei structure.

'Shoe design is what I live for,' says Charline. 'It's my biggest passion; my dream come true. With my first collection, when I saw the first prototypes of my signature cut-out wedge, I was over the moon. I'd been working on that heel for a long time, and seeing it in real life was just unbelievable.'

Charline's shoes are artful constructions, so it is no surprise that *The New York Times* once described her as a 'shoe architect'. In fact, there is more truth to that statement than one might first realize. Charline does indeed hold a degree in architecture, from the prestigious New York Institute of Technology, where she studied for five years. 'I was actually good at it, and I would definitely have become an architect. I could see myself designing posh interiors for hotels or luxury retail spaces,' she muses. 'Architecture and design still excite me greatly today. However, looking back on it, my passion for shoes always came first. My parents knew that I was obsessed with shoes. I always bought fashion history books rather than architecture books, and my notebooks were full of shoe sketches. The moment I decided to pursue it as a career they supported me,' she recalls.

After a short stint at Central Saint Martins in London learning about shoe design, Charline was resolute in her decision that this was the path she wanted to pursue. She decided to move back to Rome and to search for a job that was as close as possible to fashion. Her quest led to a position as an architect in the store-planning section at Fendi. 'That experience gave me amazing teamwork skills and provided me with a great insight into the fashion world,' she notes.

Her own studio is located in the ancient city of romance. 'The space is packed with shoes and all types of drawing tools. Sketching on my grandfather's wooden drafting table is a special treat,' says Charline. 'I love to draw inspiration from Rome, and somehow my shoes are all the more Italian for that.' Indeed, her shoes are all made in Italy, with every element fabricated by hand. Furthermore, every component comes from Italy (Charline uses only local materials), so this is a 100% 'made in Italy' brand from start to finish. 'The quality of Italian-made shoes is incomparable. Besides,' adds Charline, 'as a customer myself, I want to know where my shoes come from.' In 2012 she won the *Vogue Italia* 'Who Is On Next?' award for shoe design. A year later, one of her designs was selected for the 'Shoe Obsession' exhibition at the Fashion Institute of Technology museum in New York, curated by Valerie Steele.

Key to Charline's success is her inquisitive and determined spirit, which in practice means she constantly explores new designs and innovations. 'That will keep you recognizable and fresh at the same time. Fashion is a strong business that is resisting the pressures of a global financial crisis. It means there's still space to experiment and invest,' she states. 'That said, shoes are accompanied by rules. For a start, one has to be able to walk in them; every element has to be tested and has to be functional. That leaves you able to push your creativity only within the boundaries of the shoe's parameters.'

Notwithstanding these practical restrictions, Charline always injects technological advances into her four annual collections: approximately fifty styles. 'Metallic mirrored calf leather is one of my signatures. I've had metallics in my collections since the beginning,' she observes. 'Once I even upped the ante by inserting a metal blade into my "Prism" heel.' Another predilection that seems to be indicative of Charline's engineering approach is her desire to plate heels in every collection. 'I've experimented with silver, gold, platinum and all the metallic shades. The technique consists of dipping the heel in liquid lamina. This is then backed and the heel seems entirely made out of metal, but the lightness is that of plastic.'

And if a customer could only own one design? Without hesitation, Charline would recommend 'a high-heeled black pump, such as my "Hexa" style; a perfect example!' On a more wishful note, she says she would love to re-design Dorothy's magic red slippers for a modern remake of *The Wizard of Oz*. For now, however, she is happy keeping her customers satisfied. 'I love it when women tell me they love to wear my shoes because they catch people's attention so much that they get stopped and asked what brand the shoes are,' she shares. 'So I say to you: embrace the feeling that the shoe gives you. Feel powerful and sexy. After all, there's no doubt the world can be "at your feet".'

*www.charlinedeluca.com*

'I love how materials reflect my architectural vision. I have metallics in my collection every season, and they have now become one of my strongest elements.'

(above) Vibrant colours and rich textures define Charline De Luca's aesthetics, as seen in this image of the Spring/Summer 2015 African-inspired collection on presentation day.

*(top row, left to right)* 'Regina' high-heeled lace-up pompom sandal in burgundy suede and water snake; 'Riri Fur' ankle boot in leather, with burgundy fur application and signature cut-out wedge in plated metal; 'Michi' ankle boot in suede, with cut-out wedge in plated metal; *(above)* 'Swahili' high-heeled Africa-inspired fringed ankle-strap sandal in leather; 'Galatea Zig Zag' high-heeled cage-style bootie in leather with geometric details; 'Lula' slingback sandal in colour-block leather, with 'Prism' blade heel.

(opposite above left) Campaign image of 'Bettie' high-heeled pumps in red suede, with geometrically decorated heels; (opposite below left and right) 'Josephine' booties in suede, with multicoloured geometrically decorated heels.

(this page) 'Hexa' high-heeled multicoloured geometrical décolleté pumps in water snake, shown here in purple and yellow.

CHELSEA PARIS

Somewhere in the stratosphere between two fashion-hotspot destinations you might find yourself sitting next to a woman who is fully absorbed in the act of sketching. If you could just lean over a little, you would be delighted by what you saw: the genesis of some future best-selling shoes by Chelsea Paris. 'Whenever I'm flying, the airplane is my design sanctuary,' says founder Theresa Ebagua. 'My best ideas are conceived when I'm up in the air.' Could this be because everything began on a long-haul flight between London and Los Angeles? It was 2009 when Theresa had her epiphany. 'I was reading an article about shoe designers and how they got their start, and it suddenly hit me. When I got to LA, I immediately started researching how to go about it,' she recounts. 'I resigned from my job in computer science and embarked on this journey with a blind eye. What started as a creative hobby became a personal obsession … and the rest is history, as they say.'

One might think the brand name is related to the French capital, but in fact Theresa's business moniker stems from the names of her two daughters, Chelsea and Paris, and her operations are actually based in London. 'My design studio is a very creative space. It's very intimate, and my team has become a small and close-knit family. Sure, it's also a bit messy, with loads of leathers, moodboards and all things shoe,' she laughs.

Theresa credits the year she spent in Italy learning about shoemaking and technical design – field-training in one of the most famous design regions in the world – for cementing her resolve and validating her instincts. 'For me being a designer has emerged purely out of my passion. So it was important that my time in Italy reinforced that. Everything in my core, my breath, my blood, my sweat and my tears says "shoes". Shoe design is the love of my life. I really can't see myself doing anything else.'

Now among the UK Trade and Investment and British Fashion Award New Emerging Designer alumni, Theresa has been quick to achieve commercial and critical success. Her fierce creative approach shies away from trends, preferring to construct a recognizable aesthetic, backed up by a sharp business acumen. 'The luxury field is very competitive, but competition is good, as it makes one strive for excellence with a unique point of view. It's also why we quickly launched our e-commerce, and why our pricing strategy is to be under the competition to provide value for money, considering our shoes are all handmade in Italy using only top-quality materials.'

Theresa does not have to look far for her creative direction. Her African heritage informs her choice of colours ('my chromatic palette always pays homage to the landscape of my origins'), textures (African raffia, snake skins and printed silks), and names (Sosa, Esosa, Amor and Yuwa, among others). However, she goes beyond a literal interpretation, giving African culture a twist with roaring twenties Art Deco references (Josephine Baker is a particular icon), or more recently by exploring elements of ceremonial Japan, such as the kabuki tradition, through the use of delicate folded forms. This cross-pollination via multiple continents results in four mini-collections (Pre- and Main collections) twice a year, and affirms Theresa's mantra of 'substance over style'.

Chelsea Paris shoes are effortless, sexy and slightly quirky. 'Personally,' says Theresa, 'I like to wear things that invoke a feeling of confidence and empowerment, with a bold sense of style and self. I don't follow trends; I'd rather wear what my heart dictates.' When engaged in the process of creating the shoes, free-flowing is important at first. 'I like to keep a wide influence, then gradually, eventually, it becomes something more rounded. That's really exciting. My favourite part is editing and building the collection in order to reflect the back-story, and seeing it come together. That said,' she concedes, 'you don't always end up where and how you started.'

Theresa's favourite step in the shoemaking process is drawing the design pattern onto the shoe mould. 'I feel this is essential to limit fit issues and design execution problems. It gives you a crucial insight into the lines of the design before it's actually made. If you're a perfectionist like me,' she adds, 'it can take two to three trials to perfect a design from concept to realization.'

With each new collection a milestone, Theresa can savour her achievements, her line being distributed through the network of outposts of one of the best retail power players in the business, namely Barneys. 'If I had to advise a younger self, I would say, "Intern and work for an established brand for at least five years before starting your own brand. Learn and experience the ins and outs of shoe design. There are so many pitfalls you are unaware of that could cripple you from the start."' Indeed, a dream project of Theresa's is one day to nurture younger talents; a philanthropic mission that would see her partner with a non-profit organization to create a mentoring and support programme for people wanting to get into shoe design. Theresa is all about giving: giving back to the creative world that has embraced her so warmly, and giving an abundance of enchanting shoes to her many admiring and appreciative customers.

*www.chelseaparis.com*

(above) Cross-cultural inspiration, with designer Theresa Ebagua's African roots front and centre, for this Spring/Summer 2015 moodboard.

(opposite: left column, top to bottom) 'Jasmine' stiletto-heeled pump in African print silk, with nappa leather island platform; 'Yemi' high-heeled ankle-strap sandal in exotic snakeskin, with yellow suede; 'Yuwa' block-heeled mule in blue snakeskin and *specchio* (mirror) leather; 'Izzy' stiletto-heeled front-tie bootie in burgundy suede and calfskin; *(opposite right)* 'Efi' stiletto-heeled bootie in pewter distressed calfskin and black suede, with internal platform; 'Amor' flat ankle-strap sandal in calfskin and snakeskin; 'Ada' stiletto-heeled front-tie cut-out sandal in water snake; 'Kinah' high-heeled sandal in optic pony calfskin.

*'Designing shoes is truly an art form.
It's a way to let creations flow freely,
from sketchpad to final product.
I love seeing my ideas come to life.'*

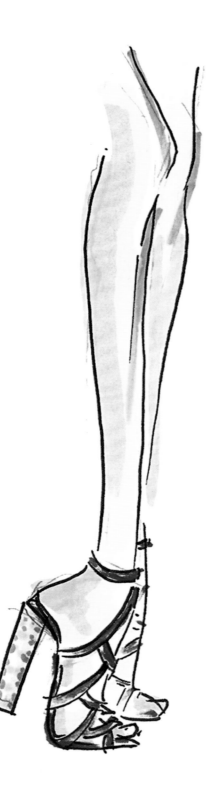

(*this page*) **Illustrations of the 'Knoyo'
sandal in red and 'Efi' pump bootie in
black, Fall/Winter 2013–14.**

(*opposite*) **'Kimi' block-heeled colour-block
pumps, shown in lemon-lime calfskin
and pewter** *specchio* **(mirror) leather with
burgundy suede tip, and in navy calfskin
and rust suede with nude snakeskin tip;
'Yemi' high-heeled ankle-strap sandals in
nude snakeskin, shown with navy and red
nappa leather; 'Jasmine' stiletto-heeled
pumps in nude snakeskin, with nappa
leather island platforms.**

DIEGO

DOLCINI

Italian chic at its height: Diego Dolcini's shoes are knockout masterpieces that have long been standard-bearers in the world of shoes fit for a (high-heeled) queen. Perfect lines, dazzling textures and hedonistic details: these shoes, with their ergonomic attributes, positively celebrate the foot. It is obvious that Diego delights in beauty, especially anatomical. At one stage, before becoming acquainted with the world of fashion, he even considered becoming a basketball player or a classical dancer: as he points out, 'both, in different ways, involve a passion for physical harmony'. By the same token, his creative approach to shoemaking fuses the best of classic style with a sense of futuristic grace.

'Since I was a child I've been enchanted by the idea of decorating the under-curve of the foot,' he remarks. 'Though I eventually graduated with a masters in fashion design, I studied architecture and art beforehand. I remember I couldn't help being attracted by the feet of Greek sculptures during art classes!' Diego's studies helped him to refine his hand-skills, and it was at university that he first started drawing in preparation for becoming a shoe designer.

Such a wunderkind could not go unnoticed for long. While still in the early years of his career, none other than Tom Ford invited him to join Gucci as accessory design director. 'That was one of the most important professional moments of my life. It was a golden period in fashion, and I'll never forget the exhilaration.' Understandably the next major milestone was when Diego founded his own company, in 1994.

There is nothing quite like a Diego Dolcini shoe, and numerous fashion icons and A-listers have been bewitched by their ultra-modern glamour. 'I can say that my shoes pick their women. Women who like a strong style or design – including powerful stars such as Beyoncé and Julia Roberts – wear my creations.' Indeed, a famous actress once wittily confided, 'With your shoes I have a good chance of finding a man tonight!' This speaks volumes about how Diego's shoes embolden as well as intoxicate, giving women the ability to feel confident about their sensuality. And, reflecting the way in which women lead multi-faceted lives, Diego revels in offering a wide range of shoes for every occasion. 'In my collections you can usually find anything from a pump (perfect for high tea) to a strappy rock sandal (perfect for your inner pop star).'

With two conventional collections per calendar year, as well as special projects and collaborations, Diego produces an average of 250 styles annually. Italian tanneries supply 99% of all his materials, and Diego underscores both Italian tradition and handcraft as essential factors, proudly stating that his shoes are 'made in Italy'. Moreover he is a staunch believer that the shoe industry is becoming ever more important, and that the purpose of accessories has evolved from being 'mere elements of decoration with a marginal use' to today, when they count as much as a beautiful gown. 'Sometimes a beautiful shoe is enough to make the perfect look,' he notes. 'I normally like to create statement shoes that have their own marked personality and consequently they can break, finish or make a silhouette,' he shares. 'I also try to achieve a balance between the right amount of creative madness and a technical and ergonomic study of the foot. I've always thought that shoes are the best expression of femininity, sensuality and elegance, but they also need to be comfortable. This is a challenge I tackle every time I create a new shoe.'

Sources of inspiration are multiple. 'A large part comes from classical music, such as Vivaldi's *Four Seasons*, but also art, fashion and people I meet. I admire the futuristic creativity of early twentieth-century shoe designer André Perugia, but also the elegant, classic taste of Salvatore Ferragamo. Creative inspiration might also come from a great movie, or a breathtaking sculpture. Anything that allows me to discover new things which give me emotion could result in a new Diego Dolcini collection.'

Ferociously against disorganization when he is working – 'I need to work in a very "clean", neat environment to maintain my concentration' – Diego can nowadays rely on getting very clear and immediate ideas, which feel emotional and instinctive, to inspire his collections. These might explore brand-new territories, or they might tap into his signature repertoire. 'From the start of my career, most of my shoes somehow always carried feathers, exotic furs or Swarovski crystals. Now I like to experiment with new and diverse materials as much as with the various soft qualities of leather.'

While Diego states that 'after twenty years I have learned that I need to follow certain rules', his creative process is clearly about experimentation and research. Two examples spring to mind: a Swarovski and fur sandal suspended in a clear Plexiglas bubble, from the 'Couture Collection', and an extraordinary black panther platform boot conceived for Madonna. These extreme designs warp our sense of balance and amaze us with their ingenuity. Perhaps they are also an indication of Diego's enduring love for the arts, and even a veiled longing to paint again, as when he was at the Accademia di Belle Arti in Bologna. 'My intention has always been to realize shoes that appear as artful dreams,' he says. We cannot encourage him enough to dream on.

*www.diegodolcini.it*

'My work is rooted in a fascination for women's feet once they are hidden. I have anxieties about how to emphasize the beauty of this part of the body; how to sublimate it within a kind of architectural structure. But I find it extremely exciting!'

ZIP

PATENT LEATHER
NERO

SOFT ELASTIC
LEATHER NERO

BLACK PANTER

*(opposite and above)* **Diego Dolcini's**
strikingly fierce, contemporary style can be
found in everything he does, as seen in his
sketches of a 'White Ceremony Alta Roma'
stiletto sandal and the 'Black Panther'
cuissarde boots he designed for Madonna.

*(top row, left to right)* 'R32091' stiletto-heeled pointy pump in satin with Swarovski crystals; 'D36007' stiletto-heeled slingback sandal in suede and silver laminated leather; *(centre)* 'S34022' multicoloured stiletto-heeled pump bootie in jade and glamour lagoon suede, lamé bronze kidskin and jade satin; 'R32029' stiletto-heeled colour-block ankle boot in calfskin, satin and kangaroo skin; 'D32090' low-heeled pump in satin with Swarovski crystals; *(bottom)* 'S34011' stiletto-heeled ankle-strap T-bar sandal in fox fur, calfskin and satin.

*(top row, left to right)* 'S34030' sculpted-heel colour-block pump in black and white calfskin and lamé bronze kidskin; 'R32034' low-heeled slingback pump in satin and calfskin; *(centre)* 'D36003' low-heeled colour-block pump in black calfskin and white nappa leather; 'D36015' high-heeled colour-block geometric-design bootie in suede and patent leather; 'D36010' stiletto-heeled colour-block open-toe bootie in black calfskin, white nappa leather, off-white suede and black elastic; *(bottom)* 'D36005' low-heeled ankle-strap pump in suede, calfskin and black elastic.

*(above)* **The name says it all: 'Bolle di Sapone', or 'soap bubble' – a concept shoe that almost makes its wearer float up in the air.**

(*above*) A take on Spartan footwear:
'Black Panther' high boots to take on
the urban jungle.

(top row, left to right) 'Black Addiction' stiletto-heeled pump in black satin, with silver spikes and heel adorned with real Swarovski crystals; 'Crystal Addiction' stiletto-heeled pump in ecru satin, with Swarovski crystal spikes and trimmings, both designed for *Addiction*, a short movie by Diego Dolcini and Chiara Ferragni; (centre) 'S35029' multicoloured stiletto-heeled sandal in black calfskin, laminated python, fuchsia laminated and geranium nappa calfskin, and geranium nappa leather; 'S35009' stiletto-heeled ankle-strap sandal in metallic bronze and gold Ayers (karung) snakeskin and black and white nappa calfskin; 'Z31033' wooden wedge sandal in mustard suede; (bottom) 'DD37006' multicoloured flat ankle-strap sandal in Ayers (karung) snakeskin and suede.

*(top row, left to right)* 'R33060' wedge ankle-strap sandal in washed nappa leather, sheepskin, calfskin and satin with Swarovski crystals; 'S35001' low-heeled pump in calfskin and woven raffia; *(centre)* 'DD37013' multicoloured ankle-strap wedge sandal in salmon suede, laminated nappa leather and fuchsia satin; 'R33001' high-heeled black and white plume ankle-strap sandal in calfskin and kangaroo, with goose feathers, brass and Swarovski crystals; 'DD37007' stiletto-heeled T-strap pump in beige satin and blue nappa leather; *(bottom)* 'Z31017' multicoloured double-ankle-strap flat sandal in calfskin and kangaroo.

E
D
M
U
N
D
O

C
A
S
T
I
L
L
O

'Follow your dreams' may sound like a cliché, but we all know that somehow this positive mantra works. Case in point: one of today's most talented shoe designers, Edmundo Castillo, the mere mention of whose name sends shoe fans, both male and female, into ecstasies. Edmundo was preparing to relocate from his native Puerto Rico to Florida, to study at Embry-Riddle Aeronautical University, when close friends decided to get married. The bride bought Edmundo a set of calligraphy pens and told him he was in charge of making her two hundred wedding invitations. 'I was set to start school on September 2nd – tuitions were paid, my dorm room was set – but Boy George was having his first ever concert in Puerto Rico on September 3rd. I had been trying everything in my power to change my departure, but had given up. My friend and I spent many nights together talking about our life plans, while I made the invitations. By then I was starting to have doubts about my career choice. When I finished the invitations and we saw how great they looked, my friend said to me, "Why are you going to Embry-Riddle? You're an artist, and you won't be happy in an aeronautical school. Tell your parents and go to that Boy George concert instead!" That moment changed everything.'

Edmundo went on to study illustration, notably with Antonio Lopez, the famous fashion illustrator who was the first to point out to Edmundo that he had a profound, hitherto-undiscovered understanding of shoe design. Shortly thereafter, Edmundo began to work for two of the most quintessentially American brands: Donna Karan and Ralph Lauren. From there he moved to Milan, where he worked for various Italian companies, including Tod's, and spent five years as creative director of Sergio Rossi. 'At the same time I developed the collections for Castañer, which is the ultimate Spanish brand of espadrilles. As a result, my creative style is a mix of everything that I learned and enjoyed doing for all those brands, where I had to stay true to their respective heritages and signatures, all the while instilling them with an international flair,' he explains. At one point, incredibly, Edmundo was overseeing about one thousand pairs of shoes a year.

Now he divides his time between Milan and New York, designing his own mood-enhancing and beyond-trend shoes, which encompass the qualities of some of his favourite things: the legacy of Antonio Lopez ('for the high sensuality of his drawings'), the work of Frank Lloyd Wright ('for its timelessness and modernity') and the sound of Pharrell Williams's music ('always fresh, everyone gets it, and it just makes you want to dance and feel good'). He constantly looks for new types of shoe to experiment with. 'As much as I love stilettos and high heels, I also love sneakers and men's shoes. I don't like to be a one-trick-pony kind of designer.'

Edmundo's creative style is currently evolving towards shoes suited for a modern way of living, in other words: 'less high drama and more great shoes that people can wear every day'. Feedback from the women who wear his designs always consists of rave reviews: 'They tell me they can get rid of any shoes in their closet, but not mine.' In turn, he encourages his customers to buy shoes only if they fit perfectly. As he once remarked: 'A perfect fit is when the heel feels lower than it really is.'

His shoes – often described as unconventional and timeless – are the kind that call for attention. 'There's a lot of the sensory world in my inspiration. I start sketching and, as I sketch, I look for more to keep the process evolving. What inspires me gets enhanced by pure fantasy,' he explains, noting, 'Music is paramount. I sketch with sounds that will add something to the sketches.'

Meanwhile, he looks for materials, builds colour cards, and starts turning his sketches into more technical drawings that will be implemented on the last where each shoe will be mounted and shaped. 'I prototype the shoes using some of the new materials and colour combinations I plan to apply. One of my favourite parts of the process is taking the scissors and starting to cut the prototype, creating new lines and new proportions. It's like sculpting. Then I go to the heel-maker, and design and hand-sculpt heels using resin or wood; we sculpt new heel shapes and continue to perfect them until they feel just right. The same happens with the last-maker when creating a new toe shape. Once the collection has been looked at, shared with and worked on by the team, we make the samples that will be used when selling a collection to the stores. When the samples are all together in New York, I then do a second edit with the team and the collection goes to market.'

Edmundo has been rewarded with the Perry Ellis Award for best emerging accessories designer, presented by the Council of Fashion Designers of America. He also won the design award for Best Travel Shoes from *Travel + Leisure* magazine, and in the same year the Style Icon Award for accessories design from *Vanidades*, one of Latin America's most popular magazines. Furthermore, in 2014, Fashion Group International honoured Edmundo with a Rising Star Award for accessories. Long may he follow his dreams, we say.

*www.edmundocastillo.com*

'I see shoes in the same way that I see a beautiful sculpture, or a great lamp or piece of furniture. I love style and people who have a unique one, but I feel somewhat disconnected from the idea of fashion and don't like to see myself as part of the trend-setting machine.'

(above) Edmundo Castillo copying a sketch onto a last, so that the factory will be able to assemble the shoe with every component in the exact position specified by the designer.

(opposite, clockwise from top left) 'Kiki' high-heeled ankle-strap tribal-inspired T-bar sandal in matt olive green snakeskin, with metallic calfskin trim; 'Raven' high-heeled pointy ankle boot in brown and white water snake and navy mesh; 'Barbi' ankle-strap flat sandal in metallic gold leather with hand-cut metal paillettes and hand-embroidered green calfskin suede; 'Astrid' high-heeled gladiator T-bar sandal in black baby calfskin, with double-buckle side straps and blue piping; 'Mary Jane – I'm Super High' slingback high-wedge sandal in chocolate calfskin and cannabis print on canvas; 'Amalia' multi-belted pointy closed-toe flat sandal with blue spots on black calfskin suede.

(opposite and above) Edmundo's stylish
sketches attest to his understanding of
ultra-glamorous femininity: here,
drawings for 'Leah' from the 'Architectural'
collection, Spring 2013, and 'Renata' from
the 'Metropolitan' collection, Fall 2011.

(above) 'Temira' sculpted cage-inspired stiletto-heeled sock bootie, with velvety black suede straps interspersed with nude mesh insets.

(opposite) 'Chad' ultra-high-heeled tuxedo sleeper pumps in burgundy suede, with towering island platforms in patent leather.

ELLEN

VERBEEK

'Shoes are our prime point of contact with the earth,' notes Belgian designer Ellen Verbeek, adding, 'They are the combination of an artistic object and an indispensable tool, and we all need them every day.' As such, Ellen's task is to ensure that her own designs are a good investment both in terms of durability and desirability. Her models offer pared-down, clean, simple lines which resonate with the style that Belgian fashion is known for. 'My shoes are definitely more Nordic, discreet and architectural. I make sure the designs are wearable, with soft cut edges and recognizable details,' she explains.

Whether the leafy twig logo embossed on the leather, the exclusive selection of natural and environmentally friendly materials (wood for heels, vegetable-tanned skins) or favourite places for brainstorming (next to the sea, or in the middle of a field), a heartfelt respect for Nature is perceptible at the heart of this designer's practice. 'The leathers are tanned according to the artisanal way – that is, without chrome – and they are anti-allergenic. This kind of leather also gets nicer with time,' says Ellen. In other words, she fabricates a product (in Italy) that is low-maintenance and that improves over time, like a good wine, which in turn suits her ethical stand against mass production and throwaway culture.

The apparent simplicity to the construction of each shoe, reinforced by the raw feel stemming from the vegetable-tanning process, is deceptive: a great deal of thought is put into each design. From the mostly Art Deco-inspired design flair to the structural engineering, via the strict selection of materials, it takes great control and patience to create a comfortable shoe with a balanced look that is far from basic. 'I know what I want and how it has to be finished. You have to feel luxury through the chosen materials and production methods,' observes Ellen. 'The time it takes to perfect a design varies a lot. Sometimes it's the first shoe of a collection that takes a long time to define, and other times it's the last one, which is added to the collection at the eleventh hour. You also have to be able to make a quick decision; you can't afford to dwell and hesitate for too long about something.'

After graduating in communication science from the Plantijn Hogeschool in Antwerp, Ellen took a drawing course for a year. Then, because she could not find a suitable shoemaking course in Belgium, she went to work at an Italian factory. It was during her year there that she decided she wanted to start creating and earning her living from shoe designing. At first, her parents were sceptical. Unsurprisingly they wanted her to obtain a suitable qualification and then get work experience at an existing company. Ellen says their reaction is totally different now that she has established her name and brand through a solid network of international retailers.

What may be surprising is that her first collection, in 2000, was in fact a bag collection. The first line of shoes did not come out until six years later. Ellen now states: 'I may be biased, but I truly think shoes are the most important component in an outfit. They can make or break a silhouette. An outfit can come to life or fall apart just because you chose the right or the wrong shoes.'

The fine line between following the rules and dodging them in order to experiment is one that Ellen gladly straddles. 'A good design requires a mix of the two. When you're totally free-flowing, there's a chance that the shoes will no longer be wearable or will be very difficult to sell. However, one has to leave the door open for unconventional ideas.'

From her office in downtown Antwerp, Ellen is only a short stroll from the main fashion district, where she likes to wander, wearing her own designs. Her personal style reveals an edgier side than one might anticipate when looking at her comparatively muted collections. 'I love contrasts: combining a very feminine style with more brutal and powerful elements. I like the pairing of a short dress with a strong boot, or a masculine look with a feminine shoe to underline the outfit.' For Ellen, this duality is, in fact, visible in her shoes: 'for example, a very thick sole under a fine, delicate upper'.

This play between masculine and feminine also highlights one of the biggest assets of her designs: their versatility. These shoes can look poised and romantic, with their slight allure of a bygone era, but they will equally enhance a contemporary urban image (imagine them with a biker jacket). Moreover, with sixty different models appearing every year, it is easy to mix and match the shoes with any wardrobe. Bottom line: when it comes to accessory making, Ellen Verbeek's holistic philosophy – the adaptability, the durability, the fine materials, the focus on quality – makes perfect sense. She paves the way for a much-needed Sustainable Style.

*www.ellenverbeek.com*

loving you all, happy to have you here with us

'Since the beginning, I have had a recognizable style. The leather line, which carries on through the wooden heel, and the Art Deco style are recurring elements that I believe make my shoes immediately identifiable.'

(above) Timeless elegance, combined with contemporary elements, define Ellen Verbeek's welcoming studio/showroom.

(left column, top to bottom) 'EV0609' bootie in dark green vegetable-tanned leather, with two architectural-design heel parts; 'EV0109" ankle boot in dark green *stampato* (stamped) velour leather and vegetable-tanned leather, with wooden heel; 'EV1409' bootie in ice-coloured vegetable-tanned leather and squared *stampato* vegetable-tanned leather, with high heel covered in wrinkled leather, Art Deco design on side; (centre) 'EV0914' high boot in iris-coloured vegetable-tanned leather, with leather strap worked into wooden block heel; 'EV1214' slim-

heeled pump in iris-coloured vegetable-tanned leather, with upper décolleté at front and pointed shape; 'EV1809' pointy boot, with slim heel covered in wrinkled leather and gaiters, in two-way-style black vegetable-tanned leather; (right) '0112EV' plateau slingback sandal in wood and tan-coloured vegetable-tanned leather, with three buckles in front; 'EV1009' high-heeled bootie in tan-coloured goatskin leather, with interior platform and wool lining; 'EV1709' pump in dark brown vegetable-tanned leather, with block wooden heel and Art Deco shape on foot.

*(left)* Fashion shot [replicated] of '1112EV' sandal on shaped wooden wedge heel and crepe sole, with three leather straps in green metallic leather and navy vegetable-tanned leather.

*(opposite)* Fashion shot [mirrored] of '1913EV' moccasin-type shoe in mustard-coloured vegetable-tanned leather, with round-shaped mustard Plexi overlay and wooden block heel.

(opposite) Fashion shot [mirrored] showing
back views of the '0808EV' sandal and the
'2008EV' pump.

(above) '0808EV' cone-heeled sandals in red
and black lacquered leather, two Art Deco
patterns on sides; '0308EV' ballerina in red
lacquered leather, with small wedge heel;
'2008EV' pumps in cream and red leather,
with fine heels covered in wrinkled leather.

ERNESTO ESPOSITO

Many would argue that a superbly designed pair of shoes should be considered a sculptural work of art. This is certainly the case with one of the great masters, whose interest and investment in contemporary art fuels his shoemaking virtuosity: Italian designer and curator, Ernesto Esposito. 'Although I would say there's not one type of woman who wears my shoes, women with creative jobs are drawn to them: art curators, gallerists, collectors, musicians,' he notes, adding, 'I've always been fully aware of the notion of "contemporary" – how life and tastes change – and, as a result, I believe my shoes are utterly embedded in modernity.'

Ernesto started designing shoes at an early age, quitting law studies mid-course, to the initial dismay of both his parents ('my mother cried, and my dad, well, he didn't talk to me for a month'). But Ernesto is one of those blessed individuals who always go ahead and do what they were meant to do. Furthermore, from the outset, he set his sights on challenging the status quo and looking to the future. His avant-garde approach is one of many reasons why over the years he has been courted by the top names in fashion and luxury.

In the 1970s he worked closely with shoe legend Sergio Rossi: a partnership that lasted over 15 years. In the 1980s he joined the team of the then-young Marc Jacobs: a collaboration that flourished for nearly ten years. He was one of the first ever designers to use a sculpted Plexiglas heel, created for Sonia Rykiel, who returned the favour by completely entrusting her shoes to him during the long period he designed for her. Further high-profile stints at Chloé, Louis Vuitton and Mugler (Ernesto particularly cherishes his memories of designer Thierry Mugler and muse Dauphine de Jerphanion) are highlights of a résumé that reads like a Who's Who of fashion. It is no surprise that in 1998 Ernesto's successes culminated in him being elected Designer of the Year by *Footwear News* and later, in 2006, receiving the unbeatable compliment of being inducted into the magazine's Hall of Fame.

After many gratifying collaborative years, however, Ernesto decided to step back and focus on nurturing his own brand. 'At one point, I was designing eighteen collections a year – more than five hundred models. Nowadays I enjoy devoting all my care and passion to my own line,' he smiles. 'I've loved every project I have ever developed, but it's always the last one I love best. The newest is always the most stimulating.' Ernesto notes that he works best when surrounded by craftsmen and technicians. 'Being together is when I feel most inspired. Besides, my "office" really fits in my backpack. I've worked in so many different places that I've become resourceful, and now my backpack is all I need to work.'

Key to the appeal of Ernesto's designs is the fact that the shoes are easy to wear. 'The first sensation that clients feel when they try on my shoes is fantastic comfort,' the designer proudly exclaims, noting that a woman should never walk on a shoe that has an incline of more than 10 cm (4 in.): 'everything else should be raised on strategic platforms to compensate'. He follows the ergonomic 'rules' when creating new models. 'The design comes almost immediately, but the construction takes some time.' The end result? 'My shoes are comfortable *and* they help make a woman's legs look beautiful. What more could you want?'

These quintessentially Italian designs might be playfully sexy (sparkles, vibrant colours, curvaceous lines) or architecturally restrained (clean graphics, a focus on a single element – a stud, a cut-out shape – rather than a cornucopia of gimmicks). 'In the design world most people think the pursuit of the extreme is a sign of good taste, but it rarely works that way. Having been a contemporary art collector for over forty years, my inspirations have always been associated with art, but when designing shoes my first thought is for the women who will wear them, as I value women totally. That's why I always focus on creating respectful, wearable designs,' he states.

The basic combo that Ernesto would like every woman to have in her closet is a black stiletto-heeled pump and a nude satin sandal. As for his favourite style detail? Embroidery applied onto versatile, light suede. Having worked as a consultant for the most important leather factories in Italy, Ernesto knows just where to find the best quality materials, and this gives him a crucial advantage when it comes to pricing and positioning his collections on the market.

Talking of market, one standout venue has to be No. 20, via Santa Caterina a Chiaia, in Naples: Ernesto Esposito's flagship store and office. From the street, it is impossible to miss. A rolling series of artworks pull customers inside: today a psychedelic fluoro-coloured butterfly-Wonderland-on-acid mural presiding over the shelves from the back wall of the boutique; tomorrow something else entirely. Ernesto likes to change the identity of the shop every six months, so as to adapt it to the theme of each new collection. 'New shoes, and a new artist as inspiration!' he cries. At this address, shoes and contemporary art – both objects of collectable and enigmatic desirability – meet in complete symbiosis.

*www.ernestoespositoshoes.com*

'I've always loved mixing a slight retro touch with the most avant-garde materials and colours, but above all I obsess about the never-ending quest for the perfect balance.'

*(above)* Ernesto Esposito likes to change the identity of his Naples boutique by exhibiting different pieces from his large collection of contemporary art. The digital artwork seen here is a collaboration with Assume Vivid Astro Focus.

*(this page)* Three sketches, three colour-ways for a design that celebrates Ernesto's love of bold and festive patterns.

*(left column, top to bottom)* **Slingback pump in geometric-design pony-style calfskin, with lacquered stiletto heel; high-heeled bi-coloured ankle-strap sandal in calfskin, with studded bow in nappa leather; Richelieu in calfskin, with shaped mirror heel and silver pin-back button;** *(centre)* **double-ankle-strap gladiator T-bar sandal in printed leopard suede, with leather-covered stiletto heel; ankle-strap boot in grained *acero* (steel) leather and suede; slingback sandal in laminated calfskin, with cork wedge;** *(right)* **cage-style ankle-design sandal in suede, with leather-covered stiletto heel; high-heeled slingback sandal in gold metallic calfskin, with black elastic bands; asymmetrical patchwork low bootie in black suede.**

*(opposite)* **'Etoile' high-heeled sandals in black suede, with Swarovski crystal star design.**

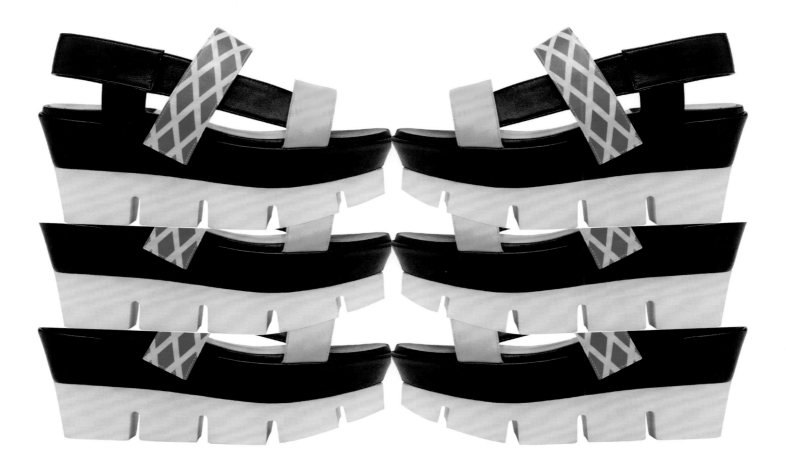

*(above)* Multicoloured wedge sandals in leather and rubber; *(right)* décolleté pumps in calfskin with black and white polka dot pattern.

*(opposite left)* Small 'Hillary' clutch in calfskin with doll-face pattern; *(opposite right)* stiletto-heeled slingback pumps in yellow calfskin with doll-face pattern.

FM
FREDARZO

To open the door of No. 11, rue de Thorigny in Paris is to be welcomed into a modern but cosy little space, where Parisian-inspired shoes are immaculately displayed. You won't be able to miss the small back office where the owner, inspirational shoemaker Frédérick Foubet Marzorati, is often busy planning his next move. In the narrow main area, two modernist chairs sit either side of an Eileen Gray coffee table, conveying the impression that discussing and trying on Fred Marzo shoes will be a sophisticated, one-on-one, confidential affair. Being the pampered recipient of the owner's expertise is a true luxury, and somehow reminiscent of the way retail once was: makers personally greeting their customers and running them through their limited-edition wares with care.

The Old World refinement somehow translates into Fred Marzo's designs. Stylistically, they are all about proportion-focused simplicity. These shoes are feminine, with a dash of sultriness; profoundly chic, with a commendable delicacy; and utterly modern in that they calibrate the right amount of retro with contemporary touches. Frédérick notes that he dislikes 'the current trend that's seeing the exaggeration of every fundamental element, such as volume and heel; in my opinion, it aims at denigrating women rather than beautifying them'. Frédérick has always loved architecture and design, and his shoemaking is a much more refined art. 'It allows me to express myself on a tiny surface, with many technical aspects being involved,' he comments. 'The fact that a pair of shoes is much more than an accessory – that it finishes, or makes, a look – is extraordinary to me.'

A vivid red line – 'a continuation of the iconic stitching of stockings' – elegantly delineates the spine of every shoe and heel, thereby guiding onlookers' eyes sensually towards the right places. The *découpe* on the side – a gentle scalloped shape that embellishes the flank of the foot – is another covetable signature, which creates unquestionable subtle glamour. 'Women are constantly on my mind when I design a pair of shoes,' affirms Frédérick, 'specifically their feet and how they sit in a pump. That's why, when it comes to high heels, I have deliberately exaggerated the arch, so that the foot can sit simultaneously at the front and the back. In return, the arch of the shoe can embrace the line of the foot much better.'

Of his design process, Frédérick explains: 'I start by contemplating potential forms and heels, if I'm not using existing ones. Then I design the different models – about fifteen per collection, including the classics and depending on the inspiration of the season. After putting ideas on paper, I design the new models on the forms. The factory here in France then makes a first sample, which we use to make any necessary adjustments. What follows is the selection of colours and skins: I have a preference for exotic ones such as python and alligator. Overall it takes about six months to get from designs to definitive samples.'

When Frédérick originally told his parents he wanted to quit school and go out and earn a living, they didn't faint but instead asked him what he was interested in. 'The following year I was studying sewing in Cannes, and that took me through for the next four years. Then I spent two years studying how to become a stylist at the Studio Berçot in Paris. While I was there, a guest lecturer – a freelance shoe designer – shook everything up. Before that moment, I hadn't realized there was such a thing as designing only shoes.' One thing led to another and Frédérick ended up working as a shoe designer at Stephane Kélian. He then moved to Christian Louboutin as a leather goods designer. His next step was three years' working full-time for luxury French house Sartore, for whom he now freelances, while running his own label.

This distinguished career path has had more than a few impressive highlights, including three seminal moments that Frédérick regards as personal successes: 'the first time I saw a woman in the street wearing one of my creations; the day that Sofia Coppola called me at Sartore to order a pair of shoes; and the time I met Sarah Jessica Parker in Paris and offered her a pair of my "Mado"s'.

'You can wear a simple dress and render your silhouette beautiful just with the right shoes,' notes Frédérick, 'but if you combine the most beautiful dress with ugly shoes, there's no hope; it totally breaks the silhouette.' One of his tips for customers is to stop and listen to their inner voice. 'If you hesitate when you're purchasing a pair of shoes, there's a big chance you won't ever wear them. But if you love them, then I can guarantee you will feel sexy.' The trick is to balance high expectations with the promise of huge benefits. 'I feel that people don't really try to understand what they're buying anymore. We have to go on teaching the importance of quality and luxury, even though we're all customers in this same consumer society. As designers of carefully made products, we have to be able to make a difference.'

With expansion projects in the pipeline (the launch of a men's line and the possible opening of another shop) and the delivery of many more desirable shoes to swoon over in the years to come, Frédérick is surely poised to make a big impression, one red line at a time.

*www.fredmarzo.com*

'Women who wear my shoes often comment on their elegance, chic and comfort. It's during the fittings that one gets the best feedback: part emotional, part constructive.'

(left) Fred Marzo's compact shop in Paris, with sleek, simple furnishings and fixtures. The shop also serves as a working studio, thanks to an ingenious back room that overlooks the main area, encouraging face-to-face encounters with customers.

(above) Sexy backs: on the left is 'Fanny', a made-to-order pump in python, with Swarovski embroidery at the front; on the right is 'Titine' in red goat suede, with a heel in galuchat (shagreen)-like printed goatskin; the N°101 stockings in the foreground are a collaboration with Nicolas Messina.

(opposite) 'Maguy' high-heeled peep-toe pump in black lambskin and mesh, on a bed of red lambskin threads – the signature symbol that adorns the spine of every Fred Marzo shoe.

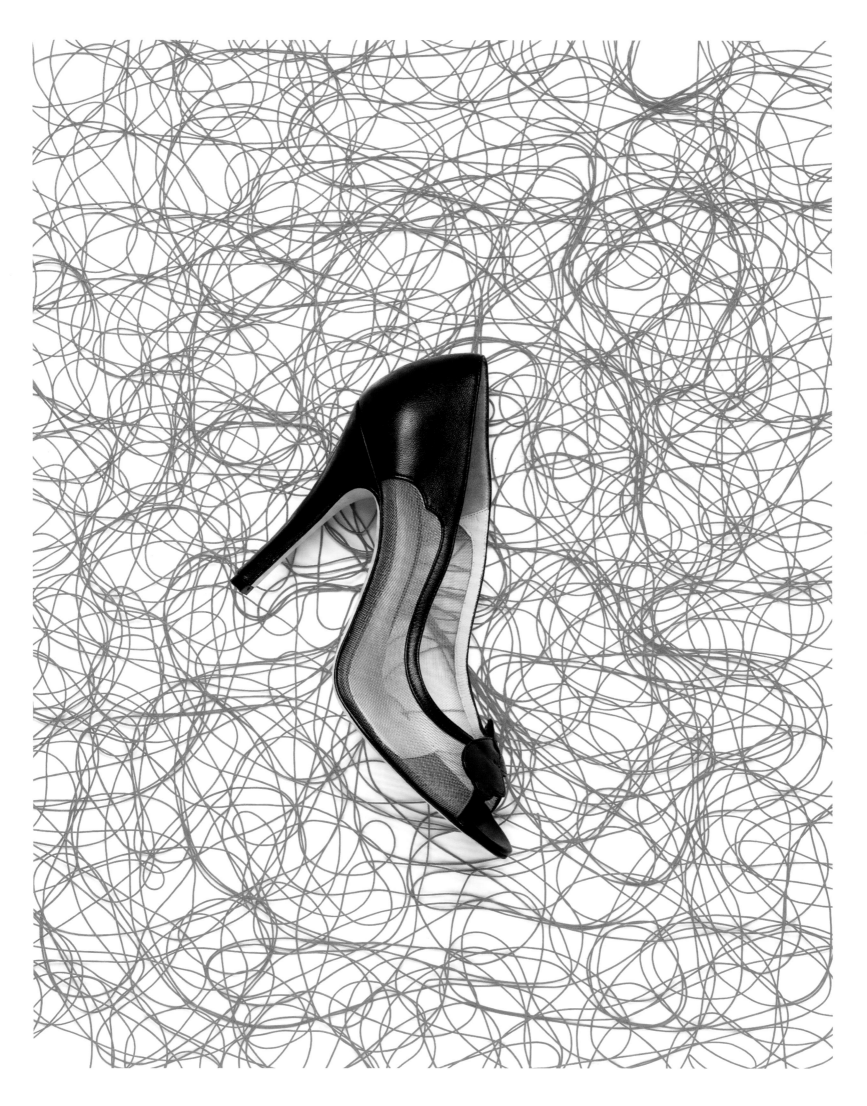

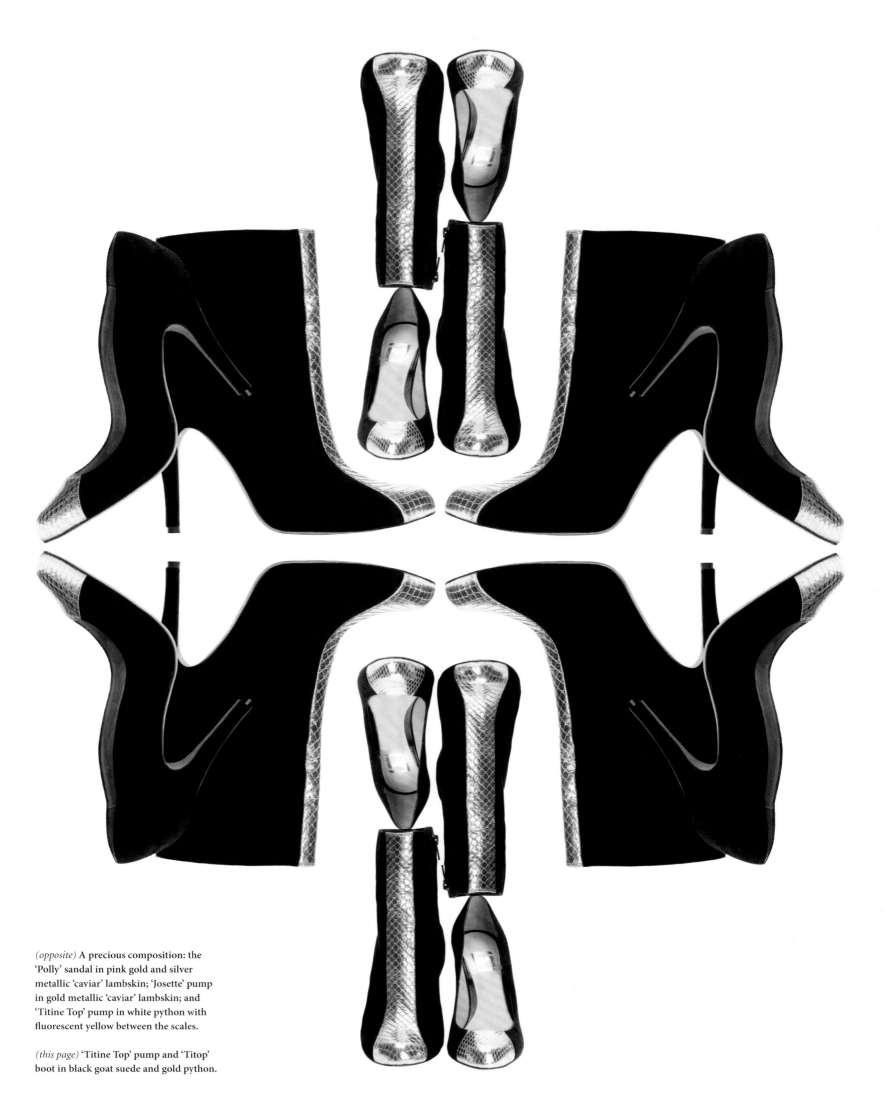

*(opposite)* A precious composition: the 'Polly' sandal in pink gold and silver metallic 'caviar' lambskin; 'Josette' pump in gold metallic 'caviar' lambskin; and 'Titine Top' pump in white python with fluorescent yellow between the scales.

*(this page)* 'Titine Top' pump and 'Titop' boot in black goat suede and gold python.

*(left column, from top to bottom)* **'Josette Caviar'** high-heeled peep-toe d'Orsay pump in metallic gold lambskin and mesh; **'Marguerite'** high-heeled peep-toe ankle-strap sandal in panacotta-coloured lambskin and mesh; **'Titine Top'** high-heeled décolleté pump in white and yellow fluoro python and mirror-varnished calfskin in acid green; *(centre)* **'Titop'** boot in crushed-paper-effect rose and white gold metallic goatskin; **'Polly'** high-heeled bi-coloured ankle-strap sandal in rose

gold and silver metallic lambskin; **'Titine Wax'** high-heeled décolleté pump in three-coloured (yellow/green/dusty pink) printed lambskin; *(right)* **'Titine Top'** high-heeled décolleté pump in pony-style calfskin (white leopard with pink and black dots), with heel in goat suede; **'Mado'** bi-coloured pump in sand and geranium lambskin, with vintage heel; **'Titine Top'** high-heeled décolleté pump in mirror-varnished turquoise calfskin.

'There's always a notion of vintage in my work, but it has evolved in a modern way. My shoes have a French touch and Parisian elegance to them.'

(this page) Ultra-feminine shapes go hand in hand with ultra-feminine names: three sketches for 'Arlette', 'Frida' and 'Titine' designs.

GIO DIEV

The case for a parallel between shoes and architecture has often been made. But you will never find a clearer representation in shoe design than in those models dreamt up by Gio Metodiev, founder of Gio Diev. Just take a look at his 'Sydney' high-rise sandal, which pays homage to the famous Australian opera house, in ultra-modern style. His shoes are not conceptual but futuristic. While conceptualism tends to favour experimentation over practicality, futurism can anticipate our desires without compromising on aesthetics or functionality. 'Imagine how unattractive the world would look if we only thought about comfort and ignored aesthetics,' Gio remarks. 'It's really all about balance and how far someone is willing to go in order to achieve their idea of beauty. That said, there's so much experimentation with shoes these days that there's hardly anything unusual anymore.' Gio's shoes stand out, with their razor-sharp lines and super-sleek allure.

'Shoes are a combination of architecture and artisanship,' he affirms. 'You need to adhere to plenty of practical elements unless you want your shoes just to sit in a museum. You have to really study the dynamics of the foot and how certain parts react when they're in motion, so there are a lot of mechanics that come into play. I also rely on the artisans at the factory and their knowledge as to how my ideas can work best in reality.'

His are shoes that seem to be pared down to the bare essentials; no unnecessary extravagance, just structural elements that are as much part of the framework as they are the actual shoe themselves. It is almost as if Gio deliberately exposes the shoe skeleton as a way to celebrate the beauty hidden within it. The slightly protruding top of a heel that gives an extra sensual boost; perfectly positioned cut-out openings that delineate an ankle; a flared vamp and counter that evoke sails: these purposeful forms all give stature to the entire 'edifice'. If you enhance those feats of structural prowess with luxurious textures (python, stingray, fox fur, patent and mirrored leather), you get a state-of-the-art product. 'I really enjoy the whole creative process,' says Gio, 'from the initial sketches, the selection of materials and the making of prototypes to the shooting of the campaign. Obviously I love shoes, but the feeling of seeing a pair that I envisioned coming to life on a woman's foot is just incredible.'

In Gio's case, the apple did not fall far from the tree. His mother has been in the shoe business for years, running her own shop in Sofia, Bulgaria, so shoes have always been part of Gio's world. 'My mother has been encouraging me since day one so there was no big revelation, but rather a sense of relief that I was finally doing something I'd been dreaming about for a long time.' That said, he did not immediately embark on his vocation. He worked first in the packaging development department at Chanel, then did marketing and PR work for brands such as Fendi and Dolce & Gabbana. 'As a result,' he notes, 'I've been exposed to a lot of different aspects of the fashion machine.'

Nothing, however, has compared to the process of creating something from scratch. 'It's the most gratifying thing for me as a professional and as a person,' he smiles. He approached the launch of his business with the same perfectionism that he has applied to his craft. It was neither a rushed decision nor a whim. He had been thinking about starting his own brand for some time, so when he decided to go ahead it was already carefully planned. 'Everything I do is done at 100% and I am very driven when it comes to my projects,' he admits. 'When you strive for perfection, you certainly find lots of challenges. I constantly think of how we can improve on an existing style, how to push the envelope further in terms of design, whether this style was photographed correctly or that leather was the right choice.'

Gio's visionary qualities are positively cinematic. 'I am a huge movie buff, so wouldn't mind being part of a movie one day – maybe producing, or even just helping a director to realize his vision in some capacity – but for now that's only a dream.' But it is possible to see how his movie-making fantasies might seep into his creativity. One can easily imagine James Bond's glamorous love interest teasing him with her 'Dion' stiletto, while the ever-present female nemesis would wear the 'Milo' style whose straps mimic barbed wire. 'It would be cool to create the shoes for a sci-fi movie,' Gio adds, 'or some kind of stage show with really out-there costumes. I recently did a pair for one of the leads in "Hedwig and the Angry Inch" on Broadway and that was a really fun experience.'

Other collaborations have included working with Swarovski on their 'Sparkling Contrasts' project, designing the shoes for American designer Sally LaPointe's runway shows, and having one of his designs featured on Madonna in her 'secretprojectrevolution' film. This shoe impresario is interested in the long game. 'Brands and businesses are not built overnight, so taking shortcuts or being a shooting star is not something we aspire to as a company. We're not very fond of fake hype.' No need for any of that here. We can count on Gio, purveyor of unique shoes, to keep brimming with ideas for many years to come.

*www.giodiev.com*

*'Architecture is a major part of women's shoe design. My models are slick, luxurious and a touch futuristic. In a way, I see them as classically modern. They are elegant but not boring; sexy but not vulgar.'*

*(left)* Gio Metodiev considering colour palettes and rhinestones for a new design.

*(opposite: left column, from top to bottom)* 'Fano' high-rise pump in beige lizard skin, with black patent detail; 'Atlas' mid-calf boot in soft grey kidskin with cut-outs and 'Blade' heel; 'Melbourne' open-toe lace-up strap sandal bootie in silver printed calfskin and lime satin, with 'Space' heel; 'Nikko' high-'Blade'-heeled pump in black patent leather, with asymmetrical inset detail in soft gold-mirrored leather; *(opposite right)* 'Dion' high-rise strappy sandal with leaf-like detail in purple suede and antique gold textured calfskin; 'Essen' cage bootie in white polished calfskin with navy suede straps and 'Samurai' lacquered heel; 'Genova' knight-inspired ankle bootie in black polished calfskin, with red kidskin cross details; 'Varna' high-heeled pump in deep green textured velvet with silver calfskin and 'Fin' details.

*(above)* **Campaign image for the 'Essen'
cage bootie.**

(above) Campaign image for the 'Nikko'
'Blade'-heeled pump in fuchsia textured
calfskin with silver mirrored leather.

(top) 'Sydney' sandal in white kidskin and gunmetal lambskin, with 'Arch' details and 'Samurai' lacquered heel; (above) 'Milo' barbed-wire-inspired sandal in black and white kidskin, with scarlet red 'Samurai' lacquered heel.

(opposite above) Detail of 'Liberty' pump in blue suede, with soft gold metal 'Wave' custom accessory ('Space' heel not shown); (opposite below) Detail of 'Medina' slingback sandal in navy blue raffia, with silver metal 'Wave' custom accessory ('Space' heel not shown).

GORDANA DIMITRIJEVIĆ

Life works in mysterious ways, and sometimes a dramatic upheaval that turns one's life upside down can turn out to be the catalyst for everything to fall nicely into place. Gordana Dimitrijević was born in Bosnia-Herzegovina and, like all her compatriots, endured the full destructive force of war in the early 1990s. Following her mother's edict that she should get a degree before committing to shoe design, she was studying economics at Sarajevo University when war broke out and put an end to her life as she had known it. 'For a while I worked as a montage assistant for a short-film production company dealing with foreign media channels, but I had to leave. When I got to France, my diploma in economics wasn't recognized.' In what turned out to be a blessing in disguise, Gordana was forced to reconsider her options, and thus she entered fashion school at last. After going to the Studio Berçot, she completed her studies with a global fashion management MBA at the Institut Français de la Mode.

'My first shoe – a sandal, created for Charles Jourdan – brought me to tears,' she recalls. 'Seeing my first sketch come to life filled me with joy. I am living proof that the adage "if there's a will, there's a way" is true.' Case in point: she bought her shop in Paris before her first collection was even designed. Call it risky or impulsive, but such actions are all about knowing exactly what you want and how to get it.

'Before becoming a stylist, I couldn't even draw because I'd been told in primary school that I had no talent for it.' Gordana, of course, went on to overcome her doubts and prove those early teachers wrong. Now she constantly draws mini-sketches on the scraps of paper that are always by her side. 'Each collection feels like the birth of a child: it's a completely different experience from the time before. My fantasy would be to design shoes without even thinking about how much they should retail for!'

Gordana creates a total of about three hundred designs every year, as she is artistic director for several other shoe brands in addition to running her own line. Each of the collections under her own name – five so far, with fifteen new models each – contains powerful architectural statements, and they are usually punctuated by contrast-coloured piping. In addition, exotic skins and strong colours that confer a futuristic edge have become signature touches. Technical elements are added, which go beyond cosmetic aspects of design: for example, the use of ballet-shoe stiffeners at the back of a model to add extra comfort and support.

No Gordana Dimitrijević shoe goes unnoticed: they exude a strong sense of personality. This is also emphasized by a marketing strategy based on the attributes of the 'femme fatale'. 'I don't believe my shoes are particularly "French" – in fact, they appeal foremost to Anglo-Saxon customers – but I was highly influenced by my first-ever experience at Charles Jourdan. The media campaigns orchestrated by photographer Guy Bourdin at the time certainly linger in my subconscious today,' she explains. 'I also like to twist one of Coco Chanel's quotes and propose, "Look at the shoes a woman is wearing:

if they are nice, the attention is on the woman; if they are bad, that's all you notice!"'

Whether flats, boots or stilettos, Gordana's creations bear identifiable constructive details that rewrite the codes of sensuality. Sharp geometrical forms are complemented by warm textures, the virtuosic use of vibrant colour and fluid feminine cues – a long tasselled lace here, a fan-shaped metallic yoke there, or simply the most delicate straps you will ever fasten. These are shoes that are made to transform an outfit, and indeed this is precisely how Gordana styles herself: 'very simple garments, often in black, paired with my shoes in neon blue or red'.

Of the shoemaking process, she observes, 'Some shoes come together quickly; some take more time. If the planning or making of a model requires adjusting more than twice, I simply drop it.' Gordana personally test-wears every shoe before it goes to production, noting, 'I don't agree with the expression "one must suffer to be beautiful". I make sure my shoes contradict this. My motto is: a good creation is one you want to buy and one you definitely want to wear.'

Working in a studio perched above her shop, usually listening to Slavic music which helps her to concentrate, she is able to eavesdrop on her customers below. She adds their invaluable feedback to her own thoughts when it comes to decision-making. Sometimes the encounters are extraordinary. One, in particular, has marked her deeply. A passer-by came into the shop, having noticed the name on the front. It turned out she had a friend who had exactly the same name. 'The customer bought a bag for her friend. Two months later I heard that the other Gordana Dimitrijević had been so overwhelmed to receive such a beautiful gift with her father's surname on it – a father she had lost touch with – that she searched for him until she found him. This moved me intensely. The fact that I contributed to reuniting these two people is just a wonderful feeling, and that's how I feel every time I listen to my customers nestled in my studio.'

*www.gordanadimitrijevic.fr*

*'Piping is an important signature of my style. The importance of line is underscored by inserting an edge between two parts. My piping is usually in bold-coloured or metallic leather.'*

(above) A moodboard combining vibrant colours and geometric patterns: the essence of Gordana Dimitrijević's brand.

(opposite above) 'Ava' high-heeled colour-block bootie in white leather and black mock crocodile leather, with black velvety calfskin piping; 'Enki' fringe clutch bag in snakeskin-printed black and white calfskin, with black leather piping and Klein Blue suede piping and fringe; (opposite below) 'Dita' stiletto-heeled front-tie slingback sandal in black suede, with geometrical cut-outs, metallic gold leather piping and black suede laces; 'Alex' high-heeled slingback platform sandal in metallic fuchsia leather, with pink vinyl and blue leather piping.

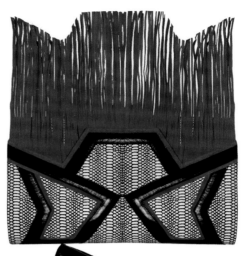

'Imagining the endless combinations of colours and textures is a drive that fuels my obsession with lines. I love calibrating details with the minute precision that can make or break a piece. It's extraordinarily exciting to be able to play with small surfaces; it's a question of millimetres.'

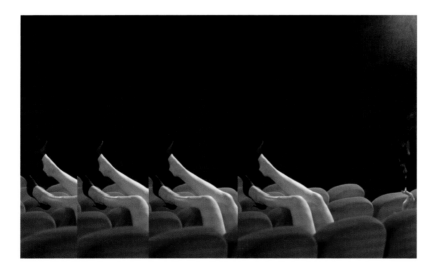

*(this page and opposite)* Sensual *film noir*-like campaign images [replicated] for the 'Byzantine' Fall/Winter 2013–14 collection, featuring the 'Charlotte' high-heeled d'Orsay pump in blue silk satin with a black-velvet-touch heel (above and left) and the 'Alma' high-heeled sandal in blue silk satin with multiple black velvet ankle straps (opposite).

*(this page, top to bottom)* 'Ea' high-heeled sandals in white ponyskin and silver, gold and white leather, with gold leather piping and leather-covered heels; 'Alex' high-heeled slingback sandals in black and white snakeskin-printed calfskin, with black and Klein Blue suede piping; 'Edgard' cuissarde flat boots in blue/green crocodile-style leather, with black leather and navy suede; 'Alma' high-heeled multi-ankle-strap sandals in sea-green vinyl, with metallic green and blue leather, and gold buckles.

(this page, top to bottom) 'Dido' bejewelled slippers in orange and fuchsia suede, with black suede piping, gold leather-covered heels and jewels made of brass and crystals (including Swarovski crystals); 'Dalida' high-heeled back-lace-tie cage-style sandals in neon blue suede; 'Dalia' high-heeled front-lace-tie sandals in blue and yellow python-style leather, with blue suede and yellow leather piping; 'Debbie' high-heeled sandals in red and blue suede, with blue metallic leather.

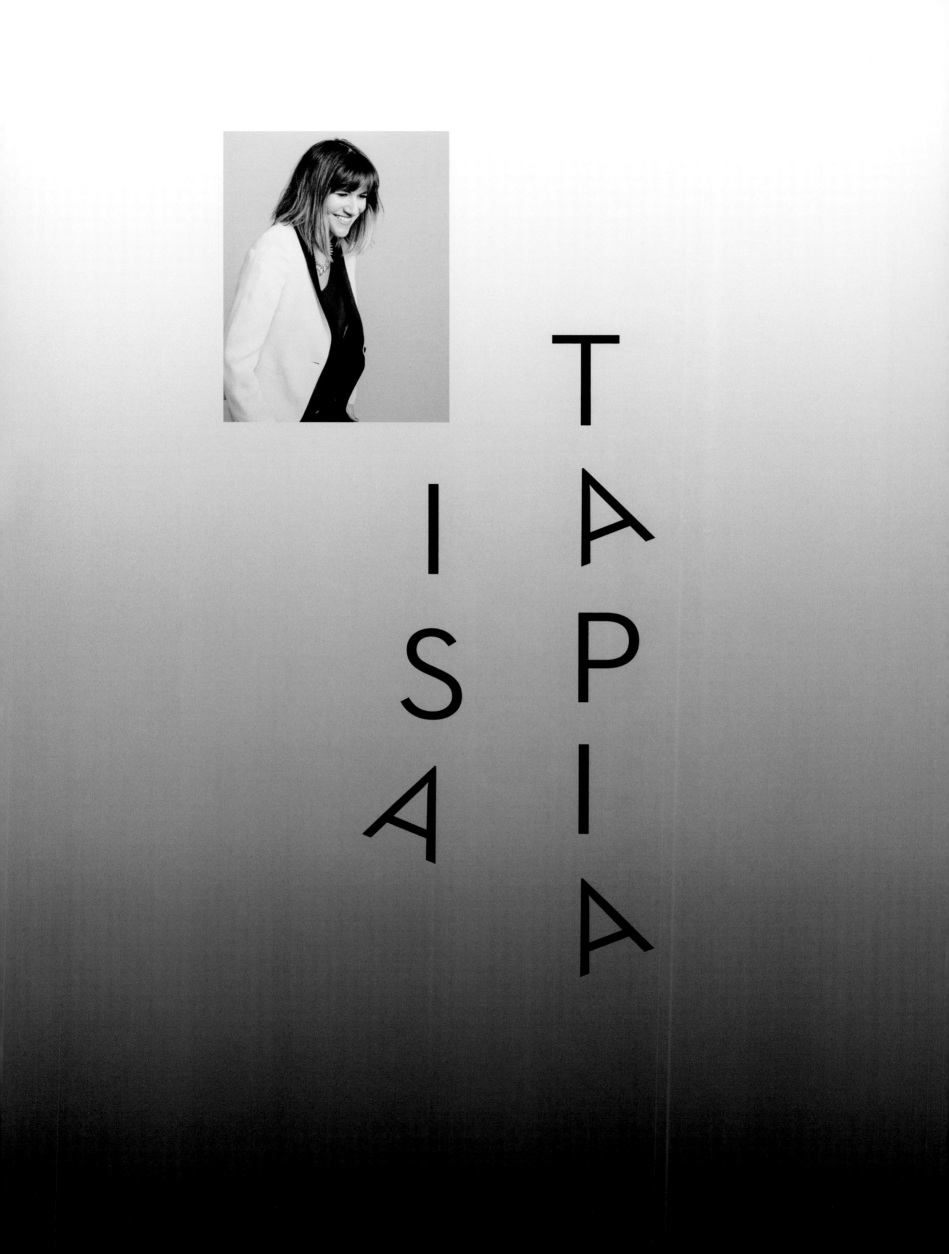

ISA TAPIA

She has a busy lifestyle; she's hyper-feminine, but with the right dose of urban grit; she's a natural when it comes to juggling sexy and casual with ease. She's a tech-savvy modern girl, who could well have been driving racing cars in another life. Depending on her mood or location, she can mix and match high with low; heels with jeans, or flats with ballgowns. She is Isa Tapia, founder of the eponymous New York-based shoe brand. She could also be all the women who wear Isa Tapia shoes with such enthusiastic devotion.

'I find it fascinating that shoes affect the way we walk and feel so much,' says Isa. 'The fit is so important: any ideas have to function, since shoes wrap around your feet, following wherever you go. Designs have to perform with precision. And it's a very different mood and attitude when you're wearing a pointy heel versus a moccasin, or a ballerina versus a sneaker.'

Isa's understanding of form and function makes her a great advocate for a versatile, free-spirited approach to wearing footwear. Her Puerto Rican origins further colour her work. These are shoes that are playful and sassy: the kind that make you want to cha-cha the night away. The Caribbean 'feel good' vibe even seeps into the choice of materials. 'I love snake skins for their texture; I also love suede because it takes bright colours so well that it becomes about the colours and not about the skin,' she observes. Finally, overtly feminine details and arabesque-style curves make these designs *caliente*!

Long gone are the days when Isa was working on logo T-shirts that she would sell to friends. She was a teenager with a burgeoning love affair with fashion. 'My mother bought me a sewing machine and *Vogue* patterns, and I started making clothes. As soon as I discovered art books and issues of *Vogue* magazine, I knew I wanted to be in fashion,' she recalls. Lo and behold, she ended up graduating in fashion design from Parsons in New York, and soon after launched her first shoe company. 'I was 23 years old and decided I was going to go for it. The first time was a flop. The blessing in disguise is that I learned a lot, and no matter what had happened it confirmed I was on the right path. Then I worked for several other companies, big and small, just waiting for the time to be right to try a solo career again.'

In 2011, opportunity knocked and Isa seized it. To fulfil her designs, she commits wholeheartedly to all the different creative elements that are required. The artist in her 'dreams of concept stories and comes up with ideas, influenced by a movie, a time period or a recent trip'. The designer part of her 'makes the idea wearable, sometimes sketching out from unrealistic concepts that have a narrative'. The artisan narrows down the techniques and crafts that will be used for the shoe uppers, 'which might be a local embroidery, or an elaborate whip-stitch pattern'. Her architect side then figures out how to construct the idea as a product, or 'how to build the last and the sole – the foundation; how to shape the curve-back of a heel'. Finally, her inner maestro 'turns the idea into an entire concept and a seasonal symphony; the collection.'

Isa always has a vision that she forges into a theme. One of her Spring collections, for example, was based on the circus. 'I was building the company, and there were so many things going on that I literally felt as if I were living in a circus. That prompted me to research circus attire and historical performers. It also explains why I've named many of my styles after famous circus women.' Isa's high-heeled shoes are systematically given female names, whereas her flats bear male names. Case in point: the 'Bonnie' pump and 'Clyde' slip-on, which are among Isa Tapia's most recognized shoes.

When it's time to build patterns from the chosen theme, Isa meets with the tanneries to see their new developments and to build her colour chart for the season. 'It takes a team to build a shoe,' she acknowledges, 'and, with the right people that understand you and what you stand for, it's like a dance.' She also spends time with technicians perfecting her patterns and shapes to build the line, making sure that an assortment of heel heights is obtained. 'Then I add my basic models in new colours to tie back to the concept. I also think about things I want in my wardrobe that I'm missing. One recent season was about slides – easy shoes I could just put on; no buckles or closures,' she says. 'I've been developing more flats and sneakers lately – things I want to wear that are comfortable. If I can make sexy comfortable, then bingo! I feel like I'm winning.'

The highs of being your own boss in the shoe industry more than compensate for any lows. 'I will always cherish the moment I saw my shoes in the stores for the first time,' Isa muses. 'I had to pinch myself. The process is so emotionally draining; it wears you down to the point of tears sometimes. But the rewards are tenfold in the end.' This is what fuels Isa's ambition … and not just to 'take on the world', but to aim way beyond. 'Collaborating with Virgin and making space shoes would be a dream project,' she enthuses. We have no doubt that Isa Tapia will reach superlative heights.

*www.isatapia.com*

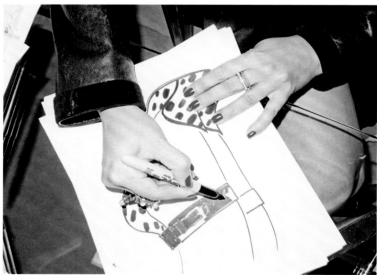

*(top left)* Isa Tapia sketching shoes at a Saks Fifth Avenue event to celebrate the company's arrival at the prestigious New York store.

*(above left and right)* A cornucopia of artefacts, personal belongings and books fill the designer's studio.

*(clockwise from top left)* 'Stefania Wave Wedge' slingback clog in kidskin suede, with natural wood platform carved in wave shape; 'Mischa' high-heeled peep-toe lace-up bootie in mixed-media (animal on animal) kidskin suede, leopard-printed exotic snake and printed kidskin suede; 'Filipa' mid-heeled swirl lace-up sandal in loopy natural tan exotic snake and kidskin; 'Lia' mid-heeled scallop-ankle-strap sandal in gold exotic snakeskin and nappa leather; 'Cha Cha' fur flat in duchess satin, with dyed natural rabbit fur; 'Nadia' high-heeled lace-up bootie in neon jacquard brocade and kidskin.

'My creative style is fun, bright and optimistic, with a bit of an edge. I like to challenge what people wear every day, and I offer a product that lifts you and heightens your sense of self.'

*(above)* 'Mischa' high-heeled peep-toe lace-up bootie in circus-embroidered kidskin suede, with metallic thread embroidery.

*(opposite, from top)* 'Carmen' single-sole wave-wedge ankle-strap sandal in kidskin suede, with natural wood platform carved in wave shape; 'Margaret' high-heeled swirl two-piece ankle-strap sandal in mixed-media (animal on animal) kidskin suede, leopard-printed exotic snake and printed kidskin suede; 'Cha Cha' high-heeled ankle-strap sandal in duchess satin and kidskin, with dyed natural rabbit fur.

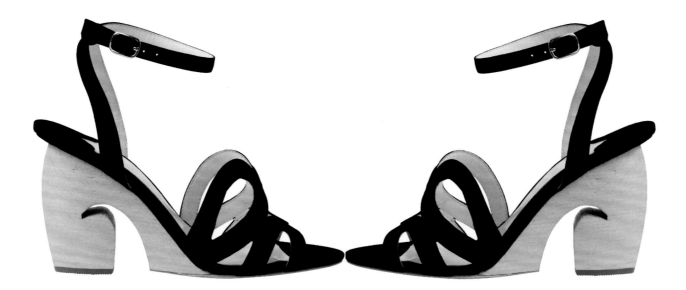

IVY KIRZHNER

As you walk down the street, you might find people stopping in their tracks and staring at your feet … if you are wearing one of Ivy Kirzhner's creations, that is. Her striking shoes are laden with intricate details and flamboyant accents that cannot go unnoticed; they are the kind of shoes that start a conversation. They actually reflect Ivy's own personal style: part free-spirited bohemian, part urban glamazon. 'I'm a Gemini, hence dual-natured,' she explains. 'Friends often say my aesthetic is global and old world, but interpreted in a very modern mode.'

This Filipino-born, New York-raised American has always been a globetrotter, intrigued by the eclectic aspects of her background and surroundings. Methods that are indigenous to different parts of the world or that were mastered in times past are her passion. 'Take the leather-woven *huarache* technique found in South and Central America,' she says. 'Its rawness and complexity still look cool and current today. I've also started dissecting Art Deco. Then again, I recently began honing in on the different eras of New York City, such as the punk movement and the glory days of Bowery.'

The back-story of each of Ivy's collections involves exploring unusual techniques and materials. For one recent Spring/Summer collection, she became fascinated by Roman, Mayan, Incan and Aztec warriors and their armour, so included several gladiator motifs that alluded to these eras. 'I like to immerse myself deeply in concepts and meditate on the vision before I jump into the outline of the detail and plan of execution for each line,' she says. 'The construction of a narrative is paramount.' Whether reticulated leather systems, complex weaving designs or metal shield-like ornamentations, Ivy revels in reinterpreting historical emblems and transforming them into sensual adornments. She also takes pains to select materials and colour palettes that are in keeping with the timeframes or geographical regions of her source material, while maintaining relevance to the fashion of today.

The signature motif that remains a constant is cloisonné enamelled metalwork on heels and platforms. 'I am fond of hardware and discovering clever new ways of incorporating it into shoes,' admits Ivy. When asked what classic shoe style she would recommend, she replies: 'Women should always have a pair of excellent low-heeled booties that can transition them from season to season. I've always believed that the cool girl wears booties all year round.'

Consummate cool girl Ivy has always steeped herself in the arts. She attended New York's LaGuardia High School of Music & Art (aka the 'Fame' school) as an art major. Later, drawn to shoe design 'because shoes are the closest thing to architecture and engineering, with the challenge of making ergonomic industrial products', she joined the Fashion Institute of Technology, where she studied footwear and accessories design. After graduation she combined her new profession with a passion for music. 'During my 20s I fronted, sang and played guitar in a progressive metal band. I was already a shoe designer working in the industry, but my band was a glorified hobby. I was

convinced I was going to be a rock star first. Similar to the way I design shoes, our music was complex and intricately layered, yet catchy,' she reminisces.

At the outset of her career, she designed for some of the most successful commercial brands of today, serving as creative director and head designer of footwear for Hervé Léger, BCBGMaxAzria and Alice+Olivia, to name but a few. These experiences opened her eyes to the market and the ways of the trade. 'My perception as a designer evolved from that time, and it made me smarter. There is really such a thing as a "good" shoe versus a "bad" shoe. Good shoes sell, whereas bad shoes end up as terrible markdowns with backed-up inventory levels!'

When it was time to finally launch her own collection, Ivy acknowledges that she had to force herself to put her name on it. 'I did it so I could push myself even harder: think harder, conceptualize better, execute with more passion. I was so anxious and getting sick from the stress, but after thirteen years of industry service it was time to take the challenge head-on, as a natural career progression. It was all self-funded with my own savings, and it felt like gambling. However, once I was able to put all the pieces together – design, operations, logistics, sales and marketing – and it proved commercially successful, it was a personal crowning achievement.' Just two seasons after her début, *Women's Wear Daily* and *Footwear News* named Ivy one of the Top 20 Directional Designers of the Year, and they did it again the next year.

'Whenever a big celebrity like Jennifer Lopez, who has a million options for designer footwear, decides to wear my shoes, I believe it is a great honour and testament to the design and product,' Ivy smiles. Her next corporate move will be in retail and product development, with an eye on positioning the Ivy Kirzhner label as an all-round lifestyle brand. 'I dream of opening a flagship boutique with a multi-line assortment, from apparel to home goods. My goal is to create a direct connection with my customers in order always to serve them better.'

*www.ivykirzhner.com*

*(this page and opposite)* This loft space in SoHo, New York, is Ivy Kirzhner's showroom/studio, housed in a former art gallery where legends such as Andy Warhol and Jean-Michel Basquiat once hung out. The high-ceilinged space, with large windows overlooking Broadway, has a cool, hip vibe: custom wall panelling, taxidermy and modern chandeliers meld with a state-of-the-art stereo system, HDMI projector, fully stocked fridge and frequent yoga sessions to form what Ivy calls 'a centre for creative freedom'.

'As a progressive designer, I enjoy breaking new ground and creating new experiences. I like to explore unconventional territories and niches, from design elements to demographics that have not been addressed before. Customers are getting smarter, more empowered and more independent in their style. This is a challenge for designers and the industry as a whole. Our job is to move with our clients. We have to offer them something new, and the product needs to be compelling.'

*(opposite)* 'Kashmir' high-heeled embroidered boots, shown here in taupe, black and dark gold soft canvas, kidskin suede and washed metallic leather, and in forest, indigo and dark gold soft canvas, kidskin suede and washed metallic leather.

*(this page)* 'Kareem' stiletto-heeled studded boots, shown here in black soft baby calfskin and rabbit fur, and in taupe natural lush kidskin suede and rabbit fur.

*(opposite above)* 'Phoenix' stiletto-heeled studded boots with enamelled island platforms and *(from left to right)* black, green and Bordeaux multi-laser geometric cuts on pony hair; *(opposite below)* 'Marrakesh' bejewelled ballerinas in dark rich gold (left) and Bordeaux (right) sea snakeskin.

*(this page: left column, from top to bottom)* 'Caballero' high-enamelled-heel harness-strap bootie in taupe and dark gold lush kidskin suede and pony hair; 'Chevron' high-enamelled-heel bead-embroidered pump in soft canvas; 'Pyramid' stiletto-heeled pump in neon pink sea snakeskin, with enamelled island platform; *(centre)* 'Roman' harness-strap wedge boot with

latticework in black luxe vachetta leather; 'Eros' low-cut flat bootie with latticework in natural luxe vachetta leather, with enamelled jewel on main strap; 'Cavalier' high-enamelled-heel bead-embroidered bootie in soft canvas and black lush kidskin suede; *(right)* 'Vishnu' stiletto-heeled slingback embossed sandal with geometric pattern and cut-outs in bone luxe vachetta leather; 'Caspar' towering 18K-gold-plated enamelled-heel T-strap sandal in black lush kidskin suede, with island platform; 'Bacchus' Roman-style flat bejewelled sandal in black luxe vachetta leather, with double-side-buckle ankle and criss-cross straps, dark gold studs and plate.

JOANNE STOKER

It is all a question of perspective: at one time Joanne Stoker considered heels of 2 cm (less than 1 in.) to be 'high heels'. Understandably, she was five years old, and the black velvet shoes with glitter lightning strikes were a Christmas present. 'I wore them for New Year's Eve to my mum and dad's house party. I remember being fascinated with high heels from a young age,' Joanne recalls. She did not, however, pursue this lead immediately. She obtained a fashion and textile design degree from Northumbria University in Newcastle upon Tyne, followed by a footwear design MA at Cordwainers College in London.

'I started out as a textile designer, but then unexpectedly took a different path into construction and architecture. Only later did I have a career in footwear, which ultimately resulted in my creating my own business. I believe I could have gone into any creative field of design, whether furniture, interiors or architecture. I really love cooking, too, and even considered becoming a chef.' Today, however, Joanne is one of the most talented independent shoe designers in the business.

Her colourful, graphic shoes are paragons of balanced proportion, with spectacular heels exhibiting a rare inventive prowess. The use of Perspex allows Joanne to engineer heels that often reference her favourite sources of inspiration – the Cubist, Art Deco and Bauhaus movements, with their use of colour blocking and modernist patterns. She has also incorporated unusual materials, such as LED lights and compressed bamboo, into her heels. These mesmerizing pieces are testament to Joanne's experimental bravura. 'People often say my shoes are like works of art on the feet, which makes me blush,' she smiles.

She creates some thirty to forty designs per year, and two collections – Spring/Summer and Autumn/ Winter. 'But I'm changing my strategy to designs that are more frequent but fewer. I'm working on transitional styles: day-to-evening shoes you can wear all year round. These will be launched four times a year,' she announces. 'I definitely encourage free-flowing in design, but my rule is that my shoes must be comfortable.' To ensure her mission is accomplished, Joanne wears her own designs – the ultimate privilege of creating your own product.

By her own account, her personal style is quite colourful, with an emphasis on precision and prints. 'I love brands such as Mary Katrantzou, Peter Pilotto, J.W.Anderson and Eudon Choi for cut and tailoring, and my latest new favourites are Rejina Pyo and Danielle Romeril. I tend to wear London designers. When I'm splashing out on a rare occasion, I love Céline and Lanvin. My wedding dresses were Lanvin and Richard Nichol,' she shares. As she says, 'It's not about throwaway fashion anymore, or one-off items; it's about timeless pieces that you can wear over and over again.' The same, of course, applies to shoes.

'The perfect shoe takes a long time to create,' she affirms. 'The sketch is the simplest part, then it takes a good three to six months to get the right heel, shape, colour, leather shades and pattern. I do a lot of research, thinking, sketching and factory work, but it's so exhilarating when I can see the final shoes finished.'

Individuality is key. 'You can't follow fashion trends if you want to create a brand. It's about creating your own signature from a vision that has to encapsulate longevity.' Another vital element for a long-term strategy lies in the choice of manufacturer. Most designers will tell you that part of their success is to have established a strong collaboration with their factories. In Joanne's case, with the exception of the environmentally certified Italian tanneries she uses because she is unable to find local equivalents, all her shoes are fully produced in the UK, with the factory just a stone's throw from her studio in Finchley.

This holistic approach, combined with an audacious creative flair, has earned Joanne a British Footwear Association design award, a First into Fashion award for her work with Jimmy Choo, who spotted and mentored her before she set up on her own, and a *Vogue* Talents award. She was even interviewed by a major luxury brand for a head of design position. 'That gave me great confidence, as they were one of my favourites,' she acknowledges. However, the most rewarding achievement of all has doubtless been her own commercial success.

'My customer tends to be a working woman, who dresses for the day and evening, and has a busy lifestyle. She likes to wear classic styles with a modern twist, and comfort is key. She's not too outrageous in her dressing, but is chic, sophisticated and grown-up.' Embodying that customer herself, Joanne has also recently introduced a range of bags to tie in with her shoe collections: one bag to suit five or six pairs of shoes. She also enjoys working with other designers and retailers. 'In the future I'd love to collaborate on a range of driving shoes with a name like Porsche,' she admits. Having always looked at improving her work, she has now finally reached a point where she is 'starting to enjoy my shoes and business without applying my own personal criticism'. Trusting one's instincts is indeed one way to flourish.

*www.joannestoker.com*

'My signature has evolved into classic shapes with architectural heels. I would like to say that I now have a heel for every woman!'

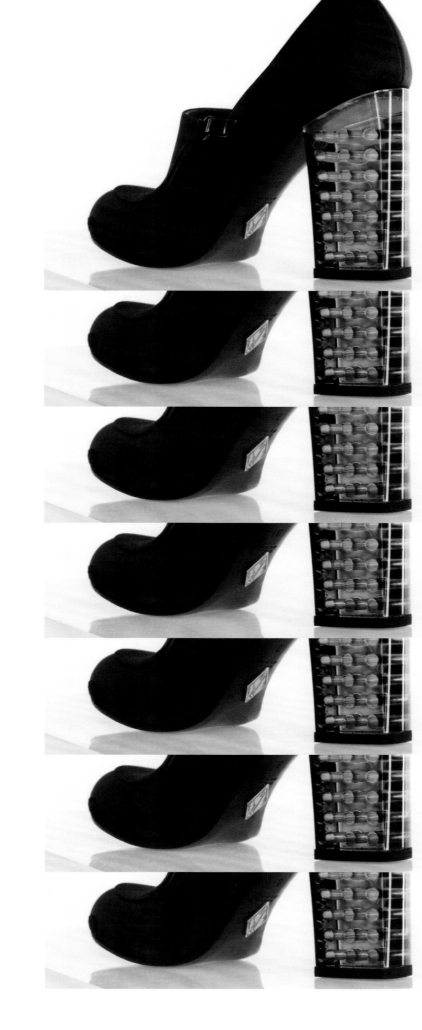

*(opposite)* Genesis of a shoe design: piece-by-piece aggregation of colour and fabric swatches.

*(right)* This fully functioning 'LED Light Heel' pump was part of a collection inspired by tower blocks on the New York skyline, Fall/Winter 2011–12.

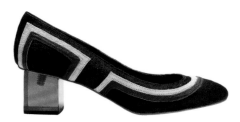

(left column, from top to bottom) **'Brigitte'** stiletto-heeled pump in pink leather calf hair with black spots; 'Loret' ankle-strap T-bar pump in brown, turquoise and mustard suede, with cut-out copper metal block heel; (centre) 'Rhonda' galvanised cube-heeled pump in orange suede; 'Ray' 1960s-style ankle boot in raspberry pink and black and white chevron printed calf hair, with suede tassels and Perspex cube heel; 'Dusty' pump with geometric pattern in navy, beige and brown calf hair, with Perspex cube heel; (right) 'Dorte' loafer-style pump in brown and black leopard-print calf hair, with cut-out copper metal block heel; 'Rhonda' galvanised cube-heeled pump in lilac suede; 'Lene' ankle boot in camel/bronze-brown calfskin, with cut-out copper metal block heel.

*(left column, from top to bottom)* 'Kohaku' platform ballerina in dusty pink denim-printed nappa leather, with striped foam sole; 'Aimi' galvanised stiletto-heeled pump in navy denim-printed nappa leather; 'Iris' curvy wooden wedge ankle-strap sandal in navy water snake; *(centre)* 'Aimi' galvanised stiletto-heeled pump in taupe grey water snake; 'Kenta' open-toe ankle-strap sandal in blue denim-printed nappa leather, with island platform in dark pink printed nappa leather and Perspex inlay block heel; 'Akane' pump in red croc-printed horsehair, with Perspex cube heel; *(right)* 'Aya' galvanised cube-heeled pump in pale pink suede; 'Saku' ankle-strap sandal in navy denim-printed nappa leather, with navy rope braid and Perspex cube heel.

*Joanne Stoker* **169**

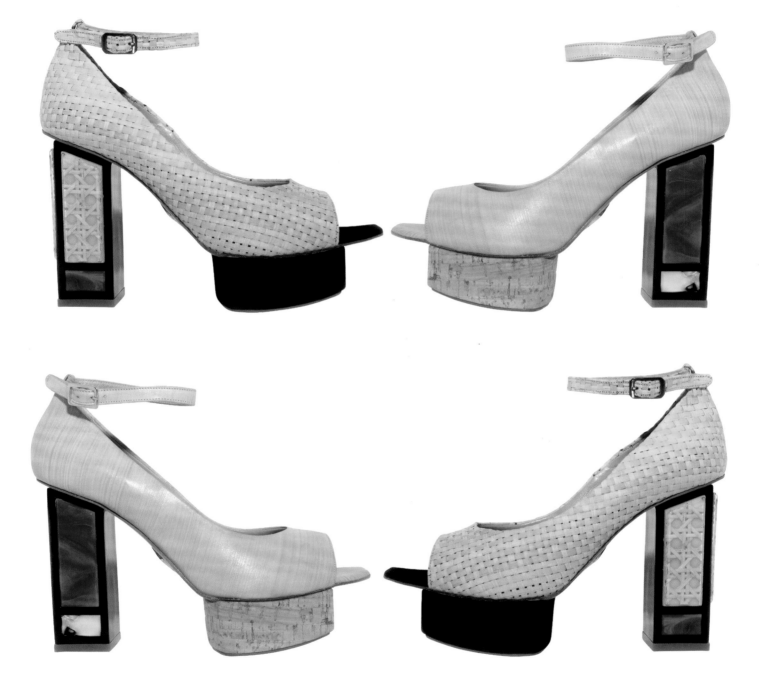

(opposite) The flamboyant 'Flamenco' stiletto-heeled folded bootie in fuchsia hot pink suede with metallic hot pink leather highlights, inspired by a dining experience at the historic Floridita restaurant in Havana, Cuba.

(this page) These open-toe ankle-strap pumps were inspired by the wicker houseboats of Kerala, as seen against their exotic backwater backdrops: 'Pink Lotus' is in blush-coloured woven-basket leather, with a leather island platform and Perspex wicker inlay block heel, and 'Tropic Lemon' is in acid lime paint-brushed leather, with a cork island platform and Perspex inlay block heel.

KERRIE LUFT

Walking on fire has never been so dazzling. Flawless flame- or twig-shaped heels adorn stylish shoes, as though they were blacksmith-forged. These either punctuate a pump silhouette (as if igniting the whole shape) or they create a beautiful contrast to the bodies of fierce booties (the one-line undulating heel like metal in fusion). Delivering harmonious proportions is key in shoe design, so this is an exercise in balance like no other. The heels and the uppers have to work in complete harmony … and in every one of Kerrie Luft's resplendent creations they do.

Perhaps it is no coincidence that this British designer's studio/apartment in Milan seems to mirror elements of her design approach. 'It's a very light, airy space,' she says, 'filled with lots of books and things that inspire me. It overlooks a beautiful courtyard with a huge tree in the centre. I love to watch how the tree changes throughout the seasons.' One immediately pictures how those branches might have inspired Kerrie's bewitching heels.

'The focus of my designs is centred on the heel, which blurs the boundaries between art and design,' she acknowledges. 'I enjoy working with metal: taking it from its raw state to a beautifully polished finish, and creating organic shapes. I like the contrast of using a material – titanium – that is both light and strong enough to create heels that otherwise look very fragile and delicate.' Since the heels are individually made from this expensive metal, Kerrie has to work backwards when pricing so that her bespoke-quality shoes are not wildly expensive once they arrive in-store. She also pours a lot of research into design, and takes time with her modelling, as each sculptural composition requires a challenging combination of physical science, art, technology and craftsmanship.

Had she not been hooked on footwear, Kerrie says she might well have become an architect. 'I've always had an interest in materials and engineering,' she notes. 'However, I've also always been very creative and have loved art since I was a child. I didn't have any expectations growing up, or a clear vision of what I wanted to do; it just evolved through time and experience.'

Obtaining bachelor's and master's degrees in footwear design from Northampton University and the London College of Fashion respectively, Kerrie worked with British accessory queen Lulu Guinness while still a student. She credits this time with giving her 'a good grounding and an understanding of luxury'. She went on to work with Canadian-British design legend, Patrick Cox. A key turning point occurred in 2011: 'I was awarded the Fashion Fringe Accessories prize. This propelled me to Paris, where I worked alongside Bruno Frisoni at the house of Roger Vivier. This experience prepared me for the launch of my own brand.'

Moving from Paris to Milan (and frequently flying back and forth to London) has certainly influenced Kerrie's vision when it comes to her designs: 'I like to work with classic colours that I imagine a Parisian or Milanese woman would wear,' she says, 'but the silhouette is the most important element, rather than decoration.' Her ultimate ambition is to have a store in Paris, 'but prior to that I'm focusing on the distribution of the collection and building relationships with some of the most iconic boutiques, department stores and concept stores in the world'.

A self-described ultra-optimistic dreamer, Kerrie holds onto an intriguing idea until she can make it become a reality. She takes pleasure in every stage of the process, but above all she enjoys creating models out of objects she finds around her studio and collaborating with the highly skilled Italian artisans in their factory ('it's amazing to work alongside people who are just as passionate about shoes').

When she is designing, Kerrie gathers a contained chaos of swatches, books and samples around her. She usually does this late at night, then the next day – with a fresh perspective – she reviews everything and edits. 'It all begins with a drawing that I've sketched from nature, and then I begin to develop the concept by creating a mock-up using wire, clay and so on,' she explains. 'Once I have a three-dimensional model I'll start experimenting in 3D software. Often it begins with just a line or a curve, and then it evolves into a heel or a pattern for the upper. The whole thing takes quite a while, as I like to experiment with colour and finish, and so I use a lot of different materials within the design. It's also a long process before I get the exact curves and lines I want.'

Kerrie currently produces two full collections a year, keeping her core signature throughout but providing variations of the heel on pumps, peep-toes, ankle boots, slingbacks and more. 'I see my designs as timeless pieces, as opposed to trend-led, so I always advise my customer to invest in a classic style that can accentuate their existing wardrobe,' she says. 'The Kerrie Luft follower is an educated customer, who understands style and fit. When she buys, it's often wisely, as she's adding to her personal style and she knows exactly where my shoes will fit into her wardrobe and lifestyle, but on other occasions she buys emotionally and cannot resist the attraction of something unique.' In which case, impulsiveness has never been so rewarding.

*www.kerrieluft.com*

(opposite above) 'Thandie' cut-out bootie in leather, with patent piping and titanium heel; (opposite below) each intricate sculptural heel is meticulously polished by hand.

(this page) 'Savona' low platform booties in black leather, with extra-fine purple titanium sculpted high heel; 'Daphne' stiletto-heeled mules in purple violet suede, with black leather leaves and piping; 'Stella' open-toe sandals in teal blue suede, with black titanium sculpted heel.

(above and opposite) **Details of the Spring/ Summer 2015 moodboard: romantic, poetic, ethereal and very couture.**

*'Customers are often fascinated by the detail within the heels, the delicacy of the design and the strength of the material. I'm always touched when they can see the Art Nouveau influences, and when they have appreciation for the concept as well as the product.'*

(*above*) 'Lily' stiletto-heeled pump in deep pink suede, with delicate gold leather ankle strap.

(*opposite above*) 'Ines' high-heeled lace-up T-bar sandal in black suede; (*opposite below*) detail of the 'Carine' black patent pump, with gold metal sculpted heel and black titanium flower.

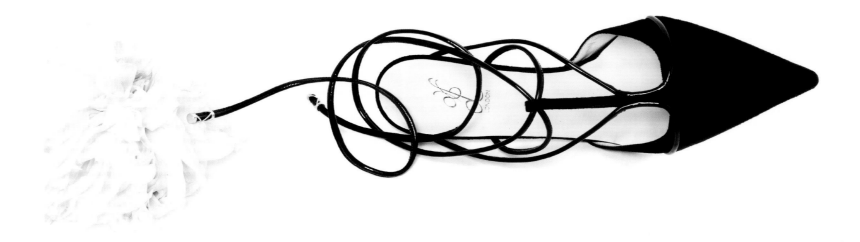

LAURENCE DACADE

Buckle up! Literally, as the fastening fixtures on Laurence Dacade's footwear are as much a signature look as they are core structural features of the shoe. But 'buckle up' figuratively, too, because to enter Laurence's world is to encounter a brilliant creative ebullience that has established this Parisian designer as a key and lasting game-changer.

Laurence had long sought to create the perfect shoe, but for many years she could not envisage shoe design as a 'job'; rather, she saw it as a private pursuit. She had started to conjure up shoes, in her 'secret and intimate bubble', as she puts it, but had trouble pursuing her passion any further. Indeed, when asked by her team to design shoes while she was working for a fashion brand, her first instinct was to give a categorical 'no'. She eventually gave in, of course, and the rest is history. 'I launched my first collection in 2003, though I feel the proper start of my brand as an organized entity only occurred later, in 2008. It took me some time to transition from what had been a very private source of gratification to an open and official stage,' she explains. 'This also suited my intention to build a legacy, rather than just have a fashion craze.'

Fashion has always been foremost among Laurence's interests. Indeed, she studied fashion design, which organically led her to entertain the possibility of studying shoe design at some stage, and also led her to start thinking about what she could do that would be more in tune with her own rhythm. It has to be said that Laurence loves fast action, and the fact that what is hot in fashion one minute is replaced by something new the next appeals to her. If you're wondering how this fits into her 'legacy' agenda, she replies that fashion dynamism – the fact that it constantly forces a designer to up their game and question themselves – positively contributes to defining a long-term vision.

Laurence has always particularly savoured the creative moments spent drawing – 'mostly at night, surrounded by scented candles, with music or a movie in a foreign language I don't understand playing in the background' – but now the process of making shoes has brought additional sources of pleasure. For one, she enjoys the time dedicated to teamwork in her workshops – 'a technical world of men', as Laurence describes it, where she delights in discussing her ideas with the artisans. 'When creating a shoe, it's all about equilibrium, precision, volume and rigour. It's a question of millimetres, and often the technicians have very set views on how to do things … which I love to challenge so that my idea gets its way,' she smiles. 'It's always exciting to brainstorm with these talented makers, and I feel they truly embrace the core identity of my brand.'

The ergonomics of shoes fascinates Laurence, 'almost in a medical way', as her drive for perfection leads her to obsess about how the foot sits in the shoe form. 'As soon as you achieve comfort and beauty in the body shape and heel, then anything goes. They are like the foundations for an architect: first get the base right, and then build around it,' she remarks.

If you could peek into Laurence's brain when the prototypes land on her desk, you would probably witness a firework of emotions. It is the one moment she cherishes above all. 'When I look at the prototype, it's as if I'm seeing the shoe for the first time, even though I've imagined it and worked on it for a while. The ultimate thrill is to feel, "Wow! I adore this design so much I want it for myself."' Of course, not all the prototypes live up to Laurence's exacting standards from the outset and, as a result, she will fine-tune until the outcome is satisfactory. Whatever the case, she does a lot of work on her prototypes in order to turn them into the designs they were meant to be.

'Love at first sight, a certain idea of *légèreté*, appeals to me. It's about the pleasure one gets from possessing an object that ultimately brings you pleasure. When a woman puts on a beautiful pair of shoes and looks at herself in the mirror, she radiates contentment,' muses Laurence. One of the best compliments she has ever received did not come in the form of overt praise, but in the form of an unexpected anecdote. She heard that a man had bought a pair of Laurence Dacade shoes … not for his female partner, but for himself. 'The way men look at my shoes is very different from the way women do. It's fascinating, and it gives me grounds to launch a specific men's line in the future,' she says. We are all grateful that Laurence has decided to share what was once an undercover passion and is now a heritage brand in the making.

*www.laurence-dacade.com*

'I have travelled a lot and am still a globetrotter today. Diversity fuels me and, in a way, it's what is infused in my designs: dualities (feminine and masculine), a variety of supple and hard materials (my favourites are kangaroo, calfskin and satin), and above all the preservation of luxury craftsmanship through multiple techniques.'

ÉTÉ 2014

Laurence Jacobs

(page 182) Sketches for a flat Chelsea pointy bootie with large grosgrain ribbon bow, Fall/Winter 2014–15; 'Gisèle' high-heeled multi-strap sandal in leather, Fall/Winter 2014–15; and 'Hope' high-heeled open-toe ankle-strap sandal, Resort 2015.

(page 183) Sketch for 'Merli Brodé', a high-heeled boot with triple buckle straps, Summer 2014.

(above left) 'Django' block-heeled Derby in white leather, with double buckles; (above right) 'Erwin' block-heeled Mary Jane low boot in white leather, with double buckles.

(left) 'Bettina' cuissarde boots in stretch calfskin, with padded heel and instep.

*(left column, from top to bottom)* 'Gwen' high-heeled lace-up pointy bootie in black and crackled gold velvet goatskin, with double-buckle ankle straps; 'Heidi' Mary Jane low sandal in ultramarine calfskin, with multi-buckle straps and wooden heel; 'Herlin' block-heeled Spartiate sandal in dusty gold split calfskin, with triple buckle straps; *(centre)* 'Gepetto' flat pointy boot in anthracite velvet goatskin, with triple buckle straps; 'Merli Patchwork' high-heeled boot in shearling and crackled leather, with triple buckle straps; *(right)* 'Merli Brodé' high-heeled boot in linen embroidered with tropical flowers, butterflies and dragonflies, with triple buckle straps; 'Hilde' Spartiate flat sandal in anthracite velvet goatskin, with triple buckle straps; 'Helie' high-heeled sandal in black creased leather, with matt silver flat nails.

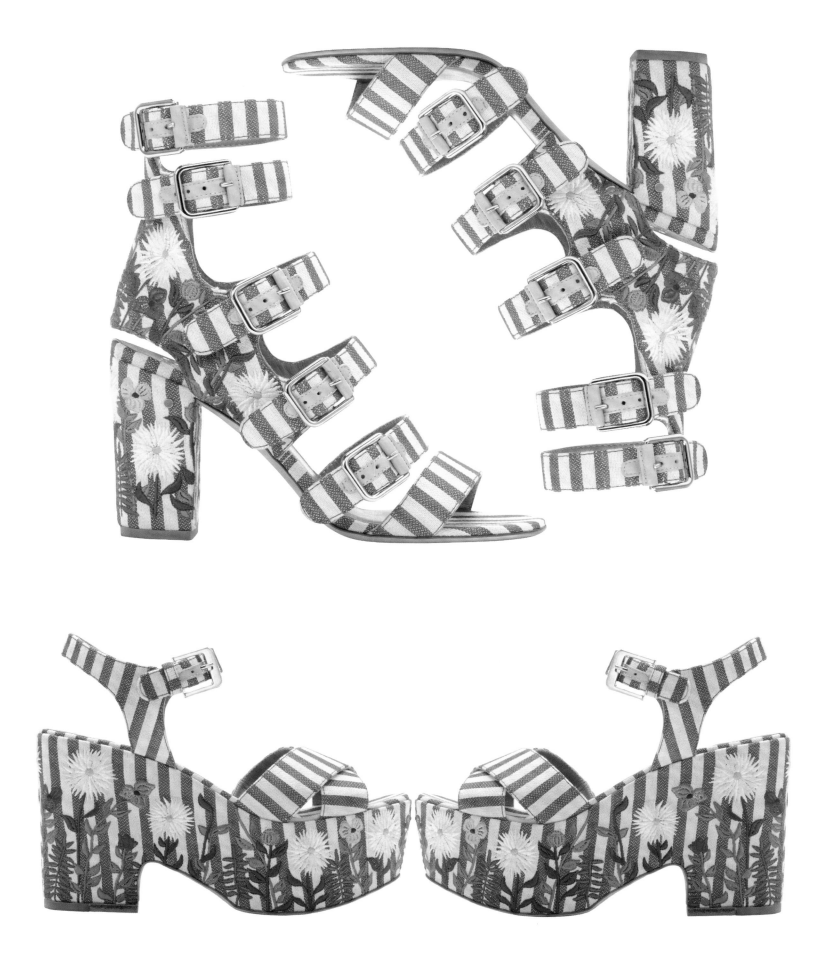

*(top)* 'Dana Brodée' high-heeled multi-strap sandals in red and white striped cotton canvas with field flower embroideries; *(above)* 'Helissa' platform ankle-strap sandals in red and white striped cotton canvas with field flower embroideries.

*(opposite)* 'Homère' flat Derby in pink and white striped cotton canvas with field flower embroideries, and 'Hermione' block-heeled open-toe sandal in sky blue and white striped cotton canvas with field flower embroideries.

OSCAR

TIYE

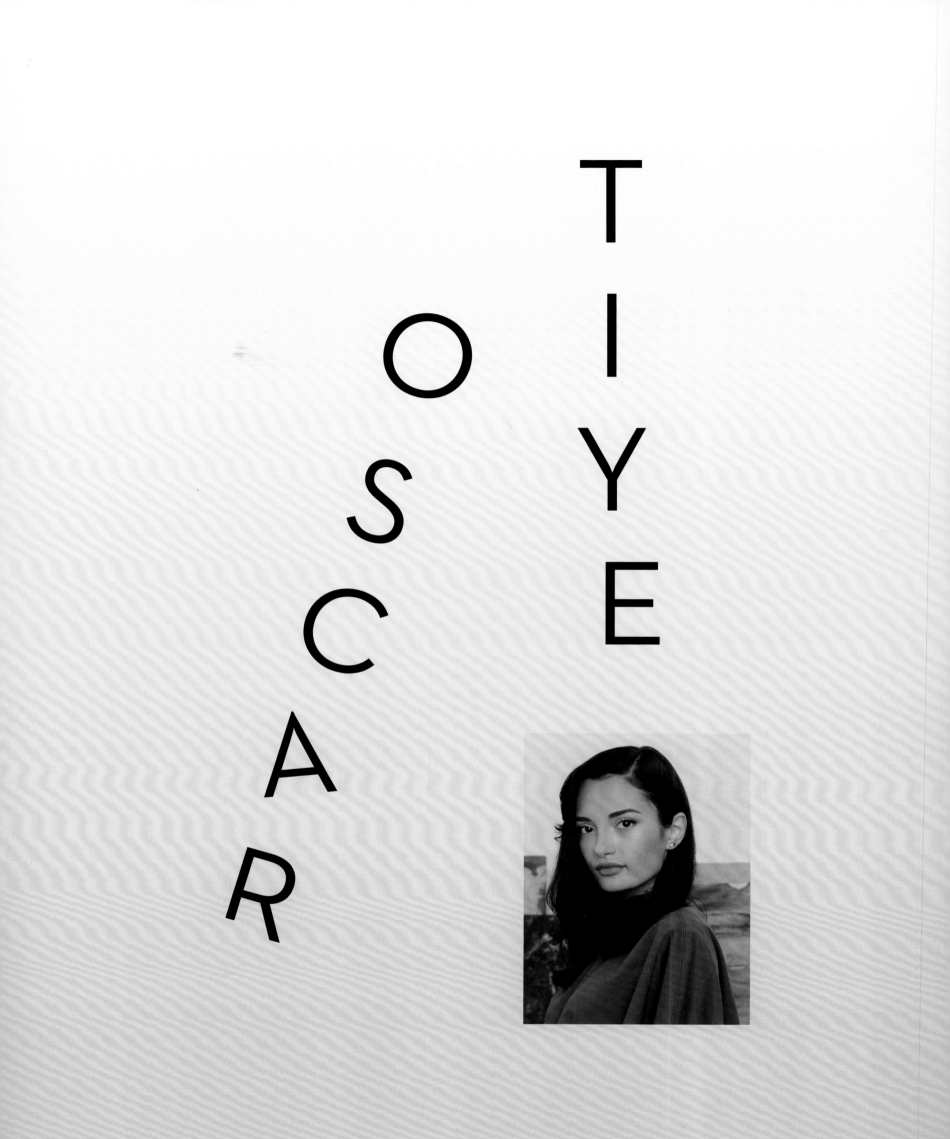

Are you stargazing over cocktails somewhere on the Amalfi coast, or venturing through Art Basel on Miami Beach, or partying with friends in Dubai? One thing is for sure: every one of these scenarios would be enhanced by a pair of Oscar Tiye shoes. Blending novelty with elegant reserve, these are the kind of shoes that stand out without screaming for attention; as a result, they are suitable for day as well as evening wear. 'I try to strike a balance between avant-garde and refinement,' states designer Amina Muaddi. 'The silhouettes are feminine, but bold.'

The designs are heady reminders of their creator's multicultural heritage. 'I'm half-Jordanian, half-Romanian, but have been living in Italy since I was sixteen. Creating Oscar Tiye has been a sort of therapeutic process; a way for me to get back to my roots. My work is a mix of Middle Eastern rich, intricate detail and Italian classic style and craftsmanship.' Amina often travels to the Middle East as a way to connect with her past and to source inspirations. Indeed, the name 'Tiye' is a reference to an Ancient Egyptian queen. In addition, the very first shoe collection was an ode to the Arab world: 'the "Casandra" shoe was inspired by the Great Mosque of Abu Dhabi; the "Jamila" by henna tattoos; "Cleopatra" comes straight from the scarab-shaped company logo; and "Zoe" features a flamingo, symbol of the sun god in the Ancient Egyptian world'.

Amina has been enamoured with shoes since the tender age of four. She grew up obsessed with fashion magazines, scouring every article and scrutinizing every photo shoot. 'At the age of nine I went to my mother with an issue of *ELLE* magazine and asked her, "What do I have to do to work there?"' Amina credits her subsequent experience as a fashion editor with shaping the shoe designer she has become today. 'I contemplate a shoe in the same way I would approach an outfit: from the colours, via the details, to the accessories. I want my designs to be cool without being too flashy.'

Amina's personal style is a difficult-to-define blend of propositions: modern, but with a dash of retro; minimal, yet a little bit gangster. 'I would never make shoes I wouldn't wear myself,' she observes. 'Having a stylist background, I also like to advise my customers on how to wear them. I like to make shoes that they can wear all the time and that are easy to match with many outfits.'

Remarkably, Amina has achieved her current status without any formal training. 'I soon realized this drawback shouldn't hold me back,' she asserts. 'I've learned so much since I started my brand. With each supplier and factory, I've felt like a baby discovering something for the first time. Now I love all aspects, from the research to the final prototype. A different kind of creativity is unleashed after the first projection on paper. The forty to fifty components in a shoe – the lasts, heels, accessories, soles – are the details I'm passionate about, and I love being in the factories and creating them with my suppliers. That's my school. That's where I've learned everything,' she enthuses. Her shoes are 100% made in Italy, including the packaging. To be precise, all the production is done in the exclusive Riviera del Brenta region, and only the finest materials are used: leathers, such as nappa and goatskin, that convey luxe femininity; high-quality suede that feels like cashmere or silk; and exotic skins, mostly python.

The Oscar Tiye trademark of vivid magenta – a regal shade symbolizing creativity – ignites hidden linings and insoles, while a metal scarab – a sacred symbol in the Arab world; bearer of happy tidings – is incorporated on every sole. 'So every time you wear a pair of Oscar Tiye shoes, a good luck charm accompanies you,' smiles Amina. 'Fittingly, the "Malikah" sandal is our most iconic shoe: it represents the logo – a beetle with open wings.' Also running prominently through every collection is the colour red. 'It's my ultimate favourite colour,' says Amina. 'It can brighten up any outfit and make it look chic. I especially love a specific tangerine-red shade that you will always find in Oscar Tiye.'

What also impresses is the use of technical tricks, such as extra padding: 'a special footbed that makes the shoes so much more comfortable'. With their sophisticated outer fretwork, Oscar Tiye designs have an almost calligraphic quality. These shoes both look and feel sensual. 'I wanted to celebrate the immense beauty of Italy, its tradition and its commitment to excellence. Exceptional attention to detail is a given, and the "made in Italy" stamp guarantees that expectations will be exceeded. That's why it's important for me to pay homage to the craftsmanship of the wonderful artisans who are so passionate and brilliant at what they do.'

Amina plans on keeping them occupied for some time to come, preferring not to dwell on past creations. 'Whenever I look at older styles, there are very few that my eye wants to continue. I'm always on to the next one, and it's my colleagues who tell me, "Wait a second! You need to repeat that shoe. We love it!"' The fact that she has already come up with best-sellers in such a short time (the company launched in 2013) is an extraordinary achievement. And it's one that didn't escape the notice of fashion editor extraordinaire Franca Sozzani, who invited Oscar Tiye to be a part of the *Vogue* Talents initiative. 'I got to show my collection to the likes of Anna Wintour and François Pinault,' recalls Amina. Oscar Tiye was even the only shoe brand finalist in the 2014 *Vogue Italia*'s 'Who Is On Next' competition. When asked for the ideal response she would like to get from those who see her designs, Amina gives a charming reply: 'I wish my shoes would make people hum, "You're just too good to be true; can't take my eyes off of you".' Consider it done.

*www.oscartiye.com*

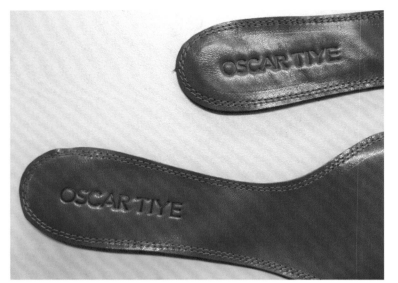

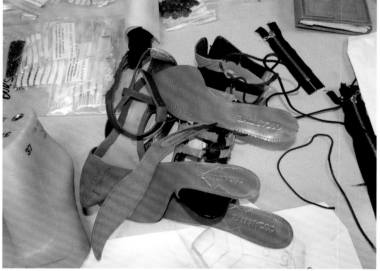

*(this page)* **A sneak peek into Amina Muaddi's studio, with the designer herself contemplating colour swatches; and glimpses of the Oscar Tiye workshop, with its plethora of made-to-measure components – stamped inner soles, lasts, gold logos, zippers – which will end up forming delicate shoes.**

*(opposite, clockwise from left)* **Sketches exuding Oscar Tiye's regal femininity: 'Casandra' lace–up cuissarde boots and 'Malikah' high-heeled sandals in black and red.**

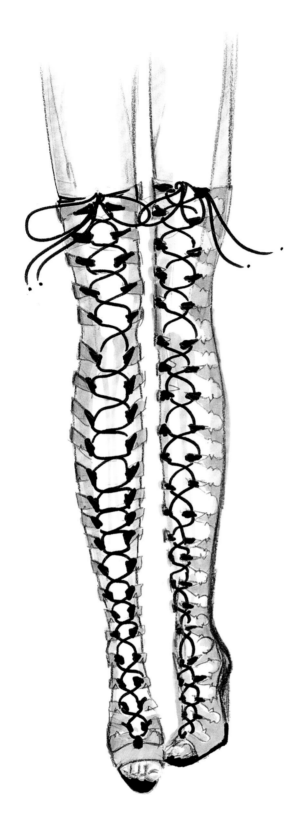

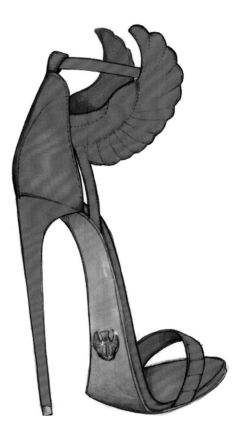

'I think every woman should have a pair of black stilettos and a pair of special shoes that will make heads turn. The first will save her from any situation in which she doesn't know what to wear, while the second will put a big smile on her face.'

*(left column, from top to bottom)* 'Malikah' high-heeled ankle-strap sandal in petrol blue suede, with wing flap detail; 'Jamila' high-heeled ankle-strap pump in white leather and python; 'Cleopatra' high-heeled ankle-strap sandal in black leather; *(centre)* 'Jamila' flat closed-toe sandal in red and nude leather; 'Malikah' high-heeled ankle-strap sandal in gold leather, with wing flap detail; 'Minnie' high-heeled ankle-strap sandal in colour-block pink and red; *(right)* 'Jamila' high-heeled ankle-strap pump in black leather; 'Amira' high-heeled pump in stripe-printed canvas; 'Zoe' high-heeled sandal in yellow and black leather, with flamingo ankle strap.

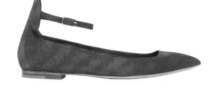

*(left column, from top to bottom)* **'Minnie'** high-heeled ankle-strap pump in black leather; 'Minnie' high-heeled ankle-strap pump in pink leather; 'Yumna' high-heeled sandal in black satin and nappa leather, with ankle cuff detail; *(centre)* **'Minnie'** flat ankle-strap ballerina in red suede; 'Malikah' high-heeled bootie in colour-block burgundy and petrol blue leather, with wing flap detail; 'Abal' high-heeled sandal in fuchsia and turquoise suede, with thorn-shaped straps; *(right)* **'Raisa'** high-heeled T-bar pointy pump in khaki leather, with black leather piping, ankle-tie collar detail and back slit; 'Amira' high-heeled pump in black python; 'Casandra' Spartiate-style bootie in mustard leather.

PAUL ANDREW

Slow and steady wins the race. New York-based Brit Paul Andrew wanted to have his own shoe collection many years before it actually happened. He had been obsessed with footwear since boyhood, inspired by his fashion-loving mother's deep closets filled with shoes ('I would spend hours studying their construction'). He is glad, however, that he chose to wait fifteen years before setting out on his own. 'I worked for several designers during that period and travelled to Italy ten times a year developing their shoes and learning the craft of shoemaking. I would certainly recommend that experience to any budding shoe designer before they launch their own collection,' he shares.

He started his design career in London in 1999 as an apprentice to Alexander McQueen, who, Paul recollects, had 'an imagination and creative need for innovation that pushed me to think and design outside tradition'. Later that year, at the urging of American *Vogue*'s accessories director, Paul moved to New York to launch Narciso Rodriguez's shoe and accessory collection: 'Narciso's ability to balance sleek lines, mature sophistication and sex appeal greatly informed the development of my own aesthetic.' Several years followed with Calvin Klein, during which time the American legend's unwavering vision taught Paul 'the virtue of staying true to one's conviction'. On Klein's retirement in 2003, Paul moved to Donna Karan, where he spent ten years working as head of design for shoes and accessories: 'Donna instilled in me the importance of functional design, impeccable quality, fit and comfort – ideals I have carried forward into my own brand,' he observes.

Now dedicated to growing his business, Paul acknowledges that his work has become more focused as he has been able to identify 'the Paul Andrew woman'. 'I am committed to designing shoes for her. She's a modern woman of the world. She's chic but not a minimalist; she's feminine but not girly; she's joyful but not juvenile,' he states. 'I strive to make a woman feel and look more beautiful, and comfort plays a major role in every shoe I design.'

Citing the great Charles Jourdan for his drive to experiment with developments in footwear manufacturing, Paul notes that he particularly enjoys working with unconventional materials. 'I had a bit of a feather moment for a few seasons,' he confesses. 'Emu feathers cascading from the ankles of bright-coloured satin booties and sandals in my Pre-Fall 2014 collection gave the silhouettes a certain life and movement. They were actually hilarious. Shoes with a personality,' he smiles.

Paul now travels to Italy every two to three weeks to oversee the development of his shoes. He usually designs close to five hundred different models each season, 'working in my Manhattan studio late at night or at weekends when no one else is there, which allows for total dedicated focus'. He narrows the list down to form a concise, well-rounded assortment of forty to fifty silhouettes, then he finalizes the shoes in Italy. 'Working with industry artisans to bring life to my collections is an essential part of my design process,' he notes.

Collaborating with French mills for novelty fabrics and Italian tanneries for one-of-a-kind skins, he works with a wide variety of textures. Suede, however, is his absolute favourite, to the extent that it features in every season. 'I've developed a special triple-dyeing process, which makes my suede significantly more durable and simultaneously brighter and more saturated in colour,' he points out. The way he balances rich textures, interesting patterns and delicate shapes may have something to do with one of his other passions – music. 'As a child, every spare moment was spent playing the piano; I even had my own orchestra in school.' Paul now designs his shoes like a musician composes a score.

He also, however, has to think like an engineer, adding hidden tricks to the internal structures of his shoes to make them more comfortable and balanced. All the while, he takes care to maintain his 'light-cum-elegant' signature. See, for example, the 'Zenadia' pump in black suede or nappa leather – a shoe that has the ability to transform any look instantly into one of sexy, chic, powerful allure. 'My aesthetic has always been decidedly feminine,' Paul notes, 'but at the time of my launch the marketplace was flooded with chunky platforms. I understood that the platform added a certain stability and comfort, but it became my personal challenge to create shoes that stayed true to my creative vision while simultaneously providing a fit and comfort that was unmatched by anything in the market.'

He has been remarkably successful in his quest. He created a pair of made-to-order slingbacks in bright red suede for actress Lupita Nyong'o that *Women's Wear Daily* subsequently named best shoes of the 2014 Golden Globes. Other highlights have included winning *Footwear News*'s Launch of the Year in 2013 and that same year being named *Vogue Italia*'s 'Who Is On Next?' accessories winner. The following year he was the CFDA/*Vogue* Fashion Fund winner – the only shoe designer to date to have been awarded this coveted prize.

Not one to rest on his laurels, however, Paul has many future projects in mind, including one that could be a fashion market game-changer: the launch of a men's collection. 'I have many ideas for men's shoes,' he says, 'and I feel there's a real niche I could fill.' Visionary and unique wins the race.

*www.paulandrew.com*

*(this page: left column, top to bottom)* 'Aristata' high-heeled peep-toe mule in black satin and suede; 'Shirin' high-heeled bootie in black whipsnake with suede and nappa leather; 'Zenadia' sculpted-high-heel pump in cobalt camouflage jacquard; *(right)* 'Shakti Soir' sculpted-high-heel pump in fuchsia satin with floral hand-embroidery; 'Lexington' high-block-heeled ankle-cross-strap sandal in matte python; 'Artemis' sculpted-high-heel slingback sandal in fuchsia and peridot python and patent leather.

*(previous pages)* Outlining the contour edges of a shoe design onto a last.

'Women are contrary creatures: ask a woman what she wants and she'll say comfort, but in my experience what a woman really desires is something that makes her feel amazing … it's a highly complex relationship!' Wryly amusing fashion favourite Rupert Sanderson rues the fact that 'there's no such thing as the ultimate killer sexy pump that feels like a Birkenstock'. If it did exist, then make no mistake: 'Women would whisper; they'd pass the word around themselves.'

Rupert's sense of humour is well matched by his pragmatic approach, which might explain why he was able to establish an international powerhouse relatively late in life. 'I started off in advertising, which I did for ten years, but it was a mistake. I'd always been interested in design. Even as a small child I designed boats, go-karts, tree-houses, school brochures, ties, T-shirts… Designs, if they're good, last a lot longer than advertising. Iconic furniture, for example, seems to have a perpetual life.'

Rupert had his career epiphany when crossing Westbourne Park Road in London one day. He suddenly realized that people designed shoes. 'I'd been fascinated by shoes and how totemistic they were, but I'd never connected the dots that there were people out there who actually drew them and got them made. It took me the width of that road to realize that's what I was going to do,' he recalls.

His previous life in advertising taught him a crucial fact: 'If you can communicate original creative ideas, then you can realize your vision.' That said, there were early challenges. 'The world isn't crying out for another shoe designer. You're not welcomed with open arms. You have to fight your way into it, so you have to have a certain dogmatic belief that you've got something to say.' Rupert certainly did, and has succeeded in positioning his brand at the high end of the shoe market: a perfect marriage of British wit and charm with the meticulous craft skills of Italy.

Taking a gamble, Rupert bought a factory in a remote Italian village at an early stage of his company's life. 'It has defined a lot of what the business stands for. And now my fondest memories are always up in the factory as the new collection is coming together. Over there, lunch is a very serious business, and even on the final day of preparation, when in the UK you'd have people tearing their hair out, everyone will break at exactly 12 o'clock for an hour and a half. It's a wonderful feeling to let go. By the end of the day – surprise, surprise – everything has come together!'

Keeping up with fashion cycles is a relentless process, but Rupert appreciates the variety that is involved and the fact that a vehicle for creative expression is offered. 'The conveyer belt that is the fashion calendar demands you get your act together every three or four months, and if you miss that you're not going to be in business for very long, but it's a great opportunity for endless reinvention.' He relishes the fast pace of change, noting that 'there's a lot of interest in things that are new and fresh'. He also appreciates the support he finds. 'Magazine editors aren't stuck for things to fill their pages with, so it's nice when respected stylists choose to shoot your product. Feeling relevant through these acknowledgments, and through customers coming in and saying they love the shoes, is always great.'

Rupert enjoys coming up with new ideas, but is careful to position them within the brand. 'You can't be restrained by what you've done before, but on the other hand what you've done before is your signature. If you deviate too dramatically from your house style, it confuses people. I think people associate what I do with a certain "modesty". My shoes aren't crazy, reckless pieces of work; they're cool, and they seem to have a sort of understatedness to them, even though they're not actually understated.'

Adding to the cachet is the signature Rupert Sanderson branding device ('a holy grail in the shoe business'). 'We have what looks like a swoop of gold on the underside. Originally hand-applied, it's now printed on every sole and is meant to represent a "benchmark"; the evidence of the hand signing off the shoe for quality. It ties in with the label inside the shoe, which is a padded gold leather ticket. I'm pleased with it: it's versatile and distinctive, without being too loud or derivative.'

Rupert enjoys his work with materials. 'Leather is versatile in itself. It takes colours and forms beautifully; it's infinite in its treatment and texture. It's a wonderful natural product that keeps on giving.' Furthermore, the constructional aspects of shoemaking – the physics of footwear – equally appeal. 'You're working with such a confined area of space, which I relish. It goes against a lot of perceptions about the free, creative, roaming mind.'

Embracing the pain/pleasure principle behind shoes – 'they're expensive; they're impracticable; they're gorgeous, essential things that women fall in love with … and that's nice to watch' – Rupert pushes himself to be the best. 'It's a good world to be in,' he says with satisfaction, 'because it mixes pure fantasy with a wonderfully practical craft.'

*www.rupertsanderson.com*

'Over the two or three months it takes to build a collection you're working very closely with the factory, the people who stitch the shoes, and the suppliers of the various materials and any hand-work that needs to be done. It's a great collaboration of individual specialists bringing together a single item. You're choreographing the final dance, and you have to keep an overview of all the different steps to keep it a cohesive piece at the end.'

(this page) Teamwork is a key word in Rupert Sanderson's vocabulary. As the proprietor of his own factory, he is able to nurture close working relationships.

'A well chosen pump is always a good sign of someone who knows how to dress.'

*(above)* **Campaign image [mirrored]** showing 'Balihai' high-heeled T-bar sandals in black and white calfskin.

*(opposite)* Campaign image featuring 'Estelle' sandals.

*(this page: left column, from top to bottom)* 'Zandy' high-heeled open-toe New York graffiti-inspired sandals in leather, with rear zip closure; 'Ohio' less-is-more pointy flats in leather, with fuchsia PVC asymmetrical overlay; *(centre)* 'Bignor' high-heeled mules in blue, raspberry and nude suede; 'Estelle' high-heeled graphic cut-out raw-edge sandals in black leather; 'Mitzy' kaleidoscope graphic raffia weave open-toe wedges; *(right)* 'Elba' high-heeled pointy pumps in python; 'Harting' high-heeled graphic cut-out sandals in metallic pink leather and mesh, with leather tie closure; 'Lintie' high-heeled Mary Jane open-toe pumps in red suede and mesh, with buckle closure.

*(this page, clockwise from bottom left)*
'Wilson' show-pony high-heeled sandals in patent leather, studded calfskin and PVC, with ostrich feathers; 'Tweeny' low-top trainers in white and camel calfskin; 'Marshal' high-heeled ankle booties in astrakhan pony, with black and white calfskin details; 'Gretel' masculine flats in leather, with side lace-up closure; 'Frances' low-heeled cowboy ankle boots in nappa leather, with a 'Varga' girl on the side elastics; 'Grenade' high-heeled ankle boots in leather, with sharp pointed toe and gold buckle detailing; 'Isolde' double-monkstrap flats in black calfskin, with frontal studded calfskin detailing; 'Salome' wedge-heeled ankle boots in leather, with gold chrome Art Deco-inspired heels; 'Urania' high-heeled T-bar sandals in satin, with snowflakes laser-etched to appear 3D.

*(opposite)* Fashion shot [replicated] of 'Pucelle' strapless sandals in white patent leather and glitter.

SIMONA

VANTH

Attract some attention with avant-garde shoes that bridge the divide between art and design. Behind company founder Simona Citarella's scene-stealing creations are strong narratives, uses of advance technology and fruitful collaborations. Let's start with the narratives, and let's mention that if Simona had not become a shoe designer she would have been a movie director. 'I haven't given up on that dream yet! I love science fiction and thrillers, and I'm writing some plots I would like to develop into short movies,' she explains. Even her shoe designs are based on characters stemming from novels or movies, 'or more often a mix of both, which I pair with something from ordinary life that I've fallen in love with'.

Unusually, Simona doesn't sketch in order to arrive at her conceptions. 'I don't trust the "virtuosity of the pencil". When I draw, everything is usually clear in my mind already,' she says. 'I think if you like what you're creating, the result will be good. If the project suits your personality, you can really push boundaries and come up with a good creation. Actually you can also produce a good creation using your professional experience, even if the project doesn't reflect your real taste.'

A believer in looking forward, Simona proceeds with ideas, even if they are ahead of their time. 'My advice is to push with determination but also lightness, and not to expect people to understand you at first. The key is to be sincere with yourself, and not to let people put you down.' Understandably she is a big fan of cult Dutch shoe designer Jan Jansen for his unstinting creativity and the fact that 'he has found his own voice … and it's a winner'.

After initial concept comes execution. 'I enjoy being in the middle of the design process,' Simona reports, 'when the new products are about to be born and there is a constructive struggle with experimentation.' Rather than sticking to tried and tested technologies, she likes to brainstorm and to explore enigmatic textural effects. 'I am a total designer,' she admits. 'I tirelessly try to translate sensations, moods and weird ideas into a real product.' Her favourite materials include micro (a synthetic similar to ethylene vinyl acetate film): 'I researched with the supplier to develop a new type with a concrete, spongy aspect, which I've been using to build wedges.' Other components she has used include plastic bubble wrap and pyrite stones gathered from the French countryside.

Simona also enjoys the technical side of construction. She has a predilection for moccasins that consist of a tubular upper with a sole stitched to the bottom. This structure makes the shoe both flexible and comfortable, and the technique can be applied to any kind of footwear. She describes her shoes as 'brutal, experimental and galactic'. In order to help harness her curiosity and imagination, she also surrounds herself with talented, highly skilled individuals who are up for a challenge.

Whether artists, artisans or industrial engineers, Simona nurtures her creative partnerships. Her multi-disciplinary approach has included collaborations with Manon Beuchot on crochet uppers and with jewelry designer Arielle de Pinto on chain crochet and the concrete wedge. 'Our unique "advanced crochet" and the stone/concrete used to build the wedges can be seen as a kind of signature,' Simona observes.

To top it all, in 2007, she and a friend opened their own shop – the now-famous WOK store in Milan. This carries international and avant-garde brands that, cinematographically speaking, Simona 'casts' and buys in for the store. She also showcases her knack for a *mise-en-scène* by art curating temporary exhibitions that take place inside the space.

She first fell in love with the creative atmosphere of a studio when, at the age of fifteen, she found herself by chance in the atelier of a famous fashion design duo. They were applying large butterflies to organza dresses. 'I think it all started there … and my butterfly tattoo is here to testify to that very first and lasting impression.' At the age of seventeen, Simona then travelled to Tokyo on her own. 'That trip cemented my resolve that working in fashion would be my future,' she recalls. While still at high school, she attended several summer courses in fashion at Central Saint Martins in London, and she followed this with a three-year fashion course at the Istituto Europeo di Design in Milan. It was not long after graduating in 2001 that she founded her own, now highly successful brand.

Every stepping stone in the growth of the business is a fond memory: the time, at a major catwalk event, Agyness Deyn was spotted wearing shoes that Simona had designed for D&G; the day her first collection was bought by one of the coolest retail stores in the world, London's Dover Street Market; the moment Simona first saw one of her shoes styled in *AnOther*, one of her favourite fashion magazines; the time Lady Gaga inquired about a design; or when the Vigevano Shoe Museum in Italy included one of her designs in their permanent collection. Judging by the speed at which Simona absorbs technological progress to incorporate stunning new elements in her cutting-edge designs, it may mean that Simona Vanth shoes even have a fan base light years away.

*http://simonavanth.tumblr.com*

'There is still so much room for things to be done in the footwear arena. I'm now more able to balance and combine both sides of my personality: the refined, luxury side and the more streetwear side. My ultimate goal is to work with nanotechnology to come up with new materials for shoemaking.'

*(this page)* **Creative essentials in a shoe designer's life: moodboard, quality swatches and books for inspiration.**

*(left column, from top to bottom)* '**Coupé**' flat sandal in sky plongé (lambskin coloured by immersion) with concrete ethylene vinyl acetate (EVA) sole and leather welt; 'Coupé' ballerina in sky plongé with black silicon drops and leather sole; 'Vanth' padded fussbett (anatomical footbed) sandal in sky plongé, wrapped with a technical net in yellow fluoro, with coconut engraved bottom sole; *(centre)* 'Medeatech' high-heeled platform sandal in nickel-coloured glow-glitter textile, wooden clog with padded white leather insets; 'Arielle' flat sandal in hair-braid-printed plongé and tiger crochet, with leather

silver sole and coconut engraved bottom sole (collaboration with jewelry designer Arielle de Pinto); 'Madame' Derby in meteorite black calfskin, with leather sole and coconut engraved bottom sole; *(right)* 'Evan' platform wedge sandal in coral plongé, with part-white lacquered wood clog sole; 'Aaliyah' padded anatomical thong sandal in nickel-coloured glow-glitter textile, wrapped with a technical net in yellow fluoro, with coconut engraved bottom sole; 'Wallabe' topsider-style shoe in cork textile with 3D coconut print, concrete EVA sole and leather welt.

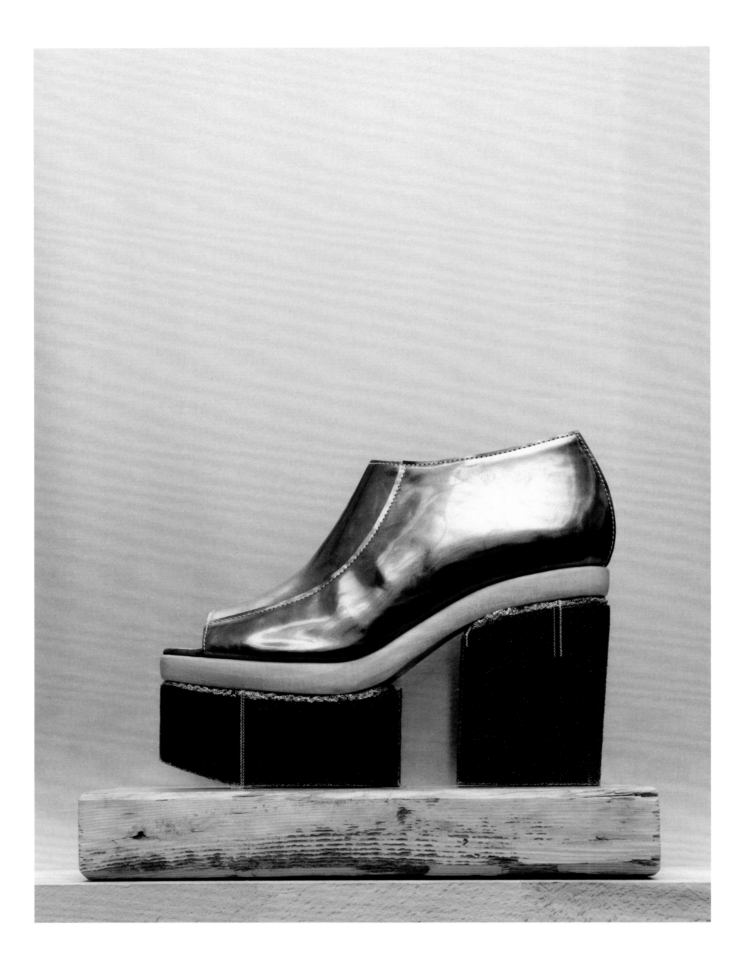

(above) 'Arielle Medea' peep-toe shoe in gold metallic melted mirror calfskin, with wood and black-sprayed concrete sole, and Arielle de Pinto gold and nickel crochet chain (collaboration with Arielle de Pinto).

(opposite) 'Poirot' peep-toe shoe in gold metallic melted mirror calfskin, with leather sole, and Arielle de Pinto gold and nickel crochet chain (collaboration with Arielle de Pinto).

*(overleaf right, clockwise from top left)*
'Madame' Derby in water-coloured
neoprene; 'Anderson' block-heeled brogue
in nickel-coloured plongé; 'Anderson'
block-heeled mid-length boot in black
*abrasivato* (brushed) leather with white
silicon elastic; 'Anderson' block-heeled
loafer in white *abrasivato* leather with
white silicon elastic: all with leather soles.

*(overleaf left)* 'Vanth Beuchot' platform
wedge sandal in crochet leather crafted
by Manon Beuchot, wedge padded
and wrapped in dark navy plongé with
clear silicon drops, and leather sole
(collaboration with Manon Beuchot).

SOPHIA

WEBSTER

The list of accolades is endless: recipient of the London College of Fashion Award of Excellence, the Drapers Student Footwear Designer of the Year, the Browns Shoe Designer Award, the Condé Nast Footwear Emerging Designer of the Year Award, the British Fashion Award for Emerging Accessories Designer… One of the 'hottest' young guns of today, Sophia Webster has achieved extraordinary success since launching her brand just two years ago, and her meteoric ascent seems to be unstoppable.

Her distinctive sense of artful whimsy appeals to a generation of fashionistas and beyond, who are well versed in pop culture references and aware that a cross-pollination between art, design and fashion is a reality. Case in point: she was chosen to create the shoes for the 'Play' and 'Shipwrecked' sections at the 2013 Victoria's Secret show and half of the shoes worn by the 'Angels' at the 2014 London spectacular (Nicholas Kirkwood designed the other half). 'It's impossible to separate the things that influenced me as I was growing up from what I do now,' says Sophia. 'All the things that were important in my youth – such as music, fashion and art – have shaped my taste, and therefore what I design. I think my shoes are quintessentially London, as opposed to British.'

Each of her sought-after Fashion Week presentations attests to her thinking outside the box. 'I try not to anticipate how people will react, as that can influence how much of yourself you put out there … and for me that's usually 110%,' she states. With seven collections a year – some four hundred individual designs – it goes without saying that Sophia is an extremely hard-working individual.

By her own admission, she is also expressive and arty; possibly a bit of an entertainer. 'I love dancing,' she says. 'If I wasn't a shoe designer, I like to think I'd be a choreographer, or a circus performer. I enjoyed acrobatics when I was younger, and I've always been fascinated by contortion.' This spirit is evident in her work. The shoes are groundbreaking, in that they are superbly conceived and made yet have just the right amount of showstopping exuberance to make them wickedly playful. The gravitas normally associated with the world of luxury is replaced by joy.

Even the list of components is delightful. 'The most unusual element I have used is probably beads with letters on them that people usually use to make personalized jewelry. I used them for my "Killer" heels!' Then there are the popsicle colours, the butterflies and comic bubbles, the veiled references to Roy Lichtenstein and Andy Warhol, the graphic constructions, and the heart symbol stitched into each sole. 'My favourite technique is hand-drawing onto an upper, then printing this onto fabric, which afterwards becomes the upper of the shoe. It's like the shoe becomes a canvas,' she explains. She also has a particular love for patent leather. 'It's the most vibrant in colour of all the leathers, and my supplier usually gets it exactly how I want it.' Trips to the factory in Brazil are a perk of the job. 'I love getting hands-on in the sampling process. It's really rewarding seeing my sketches come to life.'

When asked what sort of footwear every woman should own, Sophia makes a good suggestion: 'Pick a pair that makes you smile!' She goes further by claiming that 'every woman should have one pair of ridiculously luxurious heels that they bought on a whim, just because…'. And this is precisely why she is so in synch with her customers. She is herself a self-confessed shoe addict, and she gets what makes others tick. 'One web customer emailed in, saying she loved her shoes so much she slept with them on her pillow. That was intriguing, to say the least! To create something that can evoke such feelings is pretty special and incredibly humbling.' Sophia, needless to say, always has a pair of her own shoes either on her feet or in her bag. 'I have a huge shelf of them in my studio and a room for them at home,' she admits.

But all the fun does not distract her from the all-important prerequisites of shoemaking. 'It's really important that shoes are comfortable, wearable and beautiful. You can't really compromise on any of those elements. I do a lot of mid-height heels and some flats, too. I think as long as a woman looks at ease it will show.' Sophia also takes pains to keep her shoes at a price point that is relatively affordable for the aspirational shopper.

She first became passionate about shoes when she was on an art foundation course at Camberwell College of Art. Participating in a life-drawing class, in which the model was clothed and wore footwear, and changed outfit for every sketch, 'I realized I loved drawing shoes more than anything else,' recalls Sophia. 'From the moment I decided I wanted to be a shoe designer, I drew a shoe a day until I got to Cordwainers College.' After studying footwear design there, she completed an MA at the Royal College of Art.

Straight after graduating she became design assistant to Nicholas Kirkwood, 'which helped to teach me so much about the industry – not just about technical aspects of design, but also about running my own business'. Now she works in tandem with her husband, Bobby, who manages the company. 'Growing a business at such a fast pace is very exciting, and being able to travel the world together is obviously a bonus,' she says. 'Work never feels routine, as each season has such a different feeling. I would be worried about whether or not I was being truly creative if I ever felt my work was routine.' Absolutely no danger of that here…

*www.sophiawebster.com*

(above) As whimsical and joyful as her designs, Sophia's studio brims with pop colours and quirky objects.

(opposite above) 'Marissa' stiletto-heeled leopard pony ankle-strap sandal in electric blue patent leather, with tropical green and fluoro yellow fringe detail; (opposite below) 'Riko' open-toe bootie in orange, blue, green and black cut-out leather with serrated trim, orange leather criss-cross straps at front, black laces at back with blue, yellow and orange beads, and black stiletto heels with neon caps.

'I'm never happier than when sitting at my desk getting my ideas on paper. In designing shoes, I get to combine colour, details and patterns. Seeing these things come to life in the products and seeing the growth of the brand is really satisfying.'

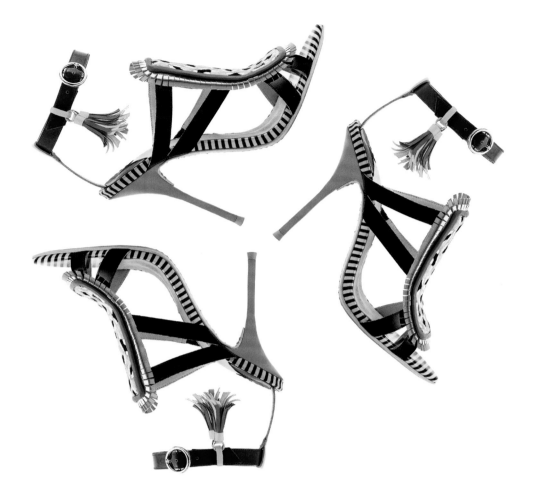

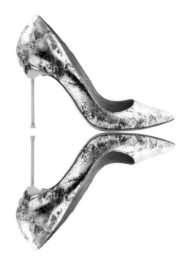

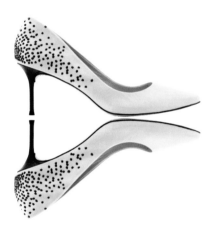

*(top row, left to right)* 'Lacey Black & White Striped' gladiator lace-up sandal in leather, with stiletto heel with red cap; 'Coco' silver rainbow leather pump with fluoro tangerine flamingo pin heel; 'Charlene' flat ankle boot in black leather and suede, with metallic silver piping and wrapped details, elastic sides; *(centre)* 'Lola' mid-heeled pump in sand leather, with embroidered neon indigo confetti dots; 'Marissa' stiletto-heeled black sandal with studding detail on a suede footplate, black patent leather straps, rose gold stud detail and ankle buckle with tassel details; 'Carrie' feather-strap sandal in leather, with multi-pastel embroidery details and stiletto heel with neon cap; *(bottom)* 'Lacey' stiletto-heeled rainbow silver leather multi-strap gladiator sandal with fluoro tangerine sole edge; 'Tia' lunar pale grey leather ankle boot, with multi-pastel feather embroidery details and stiletto heel with neon cap.

'Fun, feminine, whimsical and feisty is how one can describe my shoes. I try to convey a sense of playful luxury, and I never feel the need to please everyone.'

(above) 'I want the fairytale' speech bubble bag; laser-cut pin-heeled pale pink sandals; laser-cut open-toe black pumps with crystal details.

*(opposite and above)* **'Athena'** stiletto-heeled cuissarde cut-out boots in black patent leather.

*(right, from top)* **'Yaya'** pin-heeled T-bar sandals in red and black leather, with black and white striped sole, and ankle strap and side-buckle fastening; **'Lyla'** pointy pumps in lollipop red patent leather, with notched trim at toe upper and beaded 'killer' pin heel; **'Queen Bee'** slingback sandals in red patent leather and pale blue, yellow and black calfskin, with black and white calfskin speech bubbles and black and white beaded stiletto heel; **'Leah'** slingback sandals with iridescent mesh bow in neon and violet, patent leather strap and hologram pin heel.

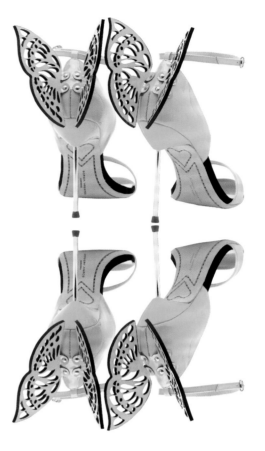

(opposite) 'Flutura' ankle-strap sandals in black, neon coral, mirror silver and eggnog patent leather, with patent leather butterfly, black patent insole cover, and silver or rose gold pin heel.

(above) Campaign image, featuring 'Catia Fur Black' sandals in black suede, with embroidered hearts and stud detail, baby pink and blue fur back, and baby blue and black beaded stiletto heel.

SUE COMMA BONNIE

There is a Korean saying that goes something like: 'Good shoes take a person to good places.' Bonnie Lee can attest to its veracity. This South Korean designer's own shoe brand, Suecomma Bonnie, has gone from strength to strength since its launch in 2003, and Bonnie has become a mogul in the making. 'Since launching my company, my dream has been to make Suecomma Bonnie a global brand. I've been participating in major fashion fairs in Paris and Milan, and I have annual brand presentations in Hong Kong and Shanghai. I hope that one day every woman around the world will have a pair of Suecomma Bonnie shoes on their shoe rack!' The latest step in her plans for expansion? 'I've launched a unisex line – Supercomma B – offering various accessories and clothing based on my original shoes. The first store opened in Korea in 2015, and I plan to launch it overseas.'

This ambitious entrepreneur originally majored in clothing design. After leaving university, she joined a well-known menswear brand and designed for them for nine years. Realizing she no longer wished to pursue a career in clothing design, she somewhat impulsively handed in her notice and headed off to Milan. 'While I was there, an old Spanish friend approached me with some nice shoes and asked if I'd like to try selling them back in Korea. That was the beginning of my "shoe agent" business,' she explains. 'As a shoe agent, there were many occasions on which I had to change the design to suit the buyers' demands. That led me to draw shoes and, as a result, I realized I wanted to make shoes that I wanted to wear.'

Shoe design was not a subject that was offered at university in Korea, however, so Bonnie resorted to working at a shoe-manufacturing factory, serving coffee to the technicians, in order to learn how to create patterns and stitch. 'That was the first stepping-stone in my transformation into a fully fledged shoe designer,' she observes.

The launch of Suecomma Bonnie coincided with the opening of the label's first boutique in Seoul. 'I'd often passed a little flower shop in a semi-basement in an alley in Cheongdam-dong and thought it would be a great spot for a shoe store. One day I saw that the spot was vacant and my heart started pounding. I decided to sign the contract on the spot, and right there and then was the beginning of the first Suecomma Bonnie store.'

For the first few days, most of the revenue was generated by Bonnie's friends and acquaintances. Everything changed, however, when an elegant woman came into the store one day. 'She was my real "first" customer. She complimented my designs and bought several pairs. She even took her Jimmy Choos off and wore my designs out of the store!' Ever since then Bonnie has been committed to creating shoes for those who crave beautiful design.

'Feeling my skin against quality leather; feeling high heels elevating my body; feeling the excitement of seeing a design coming to life: these are the moments I love,' she states. A fast-paced personality, she does not linger too long if a new design idea pops into her head. 'I make a sketch and go straight to the factory to make a sample.' That said, she acknowledges that finalizing a design is often a difficult process, and if there is a lot of detail it may even take several months. 'Excluding special items, it usually takes me one week to design and create a final sample, but I don't have a time limit when it comes to developing new heels or materials.'

With a total of four collections per year – over one hundred styles, plus an additional sixty just for overseas markets – the Suecomma Bonnie brand offers a varied and comprehensive range, from high heels and flip-flops to sneakers and boots. These designs for every occasion share company hallmarks, not just in terms of exhibiting femininity, sexiness and glamour, but also in terms of functional aspects such as interior heels in sneakers, or hidden stitching.

'My inspiration comes from modern-day women, whether walking down the street, at work, or on vacation,' she says. 'I also look at women in clubs who are listening to music. Women always wear their favourite shoes to clubs and parties, because those shoes have to be the most fabulous and the most comfortable. At those venues, there is always music and women with different tastes, and that's where I sometimes get my inspiration.'

South Korea's ultra-connectivity and hyper-modern consumerism must also surely impact on a designer's work. Bonnie agrees and acknowledges that Korean consumers are the pickiest, and that while most Korean women are known to prefer feminine and simple looks they cannot overlook bold and sexy aspects. 'No element should be overdone or underdone, and you should present both popular appeal and originality. Korean consumers have also recently started referring to "price performance". They will never open their wallets unless both quality and wearability are satisfied. It's fair to say that Korean consumers are better informed than many designers when it comes to products and services, due to the Internet and networking.' This heritage and challenge fuel Bonnie's desire to stay in pole position: she's always a step ahead of the game.

*www.suecommabonnie.com*

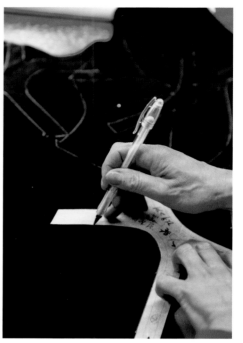

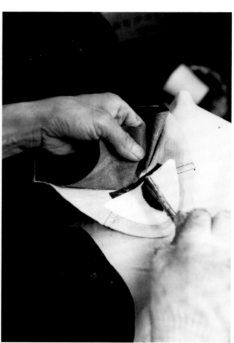

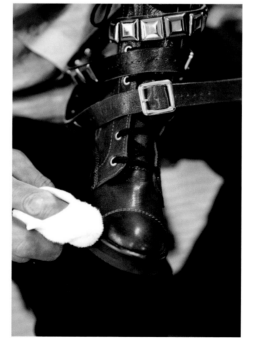

*(this page)* The creation of top-quality samples: selecting the best fabrics; working with a pattern; trimming leather; moulding a toe; tailoring strips of leather; and wiping off pen marks.

*(opposite: left column, top to bottom)* Platform open-toe bootie in black leather, with pleated crown; flat slingback bejewelled T-bar sandal in printed leather and fabric, with rubber sole; high-heeled ankle boot in black suede, with frilly fur; *(centre)* high-heeled open-toe bootie in two-tone leather, with clear rhinestones; 'Climbi in Green' walking boot in leather and fabric, with platform heel; high-heeled slingback bejewelled T-bar sandal in printed leather and fabric, with rubber sole and island platform; *(right)* 'Climbi in Gold' walking boot in leather and fabric, with platform heel; peep-toe ankle boot in printed leather, with PVC lettering and wedge; high-heeled open-toe bejewelled bootie in khaki satin.

(page 234) 'Eva' sandals (platform and flat versions) in leather and fabric [roller skates included for styling only].

(page 235) 'Spike G' fussbett (anatomical footbed) sandals in silver mirror leather, with gold studs.

(top) Slingback printed wedge in white neoprene, with bejewelled T-bar.

(above) Slingback multi-strap bejewelled wedge in printed and red fabric.

'It's important to keep things fresh. That's why I often collaborate with artists, celebrities and designers in different fields. I like to try out new arenas I've never been involved in before.'

'Shoes have a distinctive charm and power, which cannot be replaced by any other item. That's why you should look after your shoes as if they were part of your own body!'

*(above)* **Runway image from the presentation of the 'Sporty Glam' Spring/Summer 2013 collection.**

*(above right)* **Backstage image from the Fall/Winter 2012–13 presentation.**

# TABITHA SIMMONS

Can one have it all? After meeting Tabitha Simmons, it seems the answer is, 'Yes, and some more.' Shoe designer, stylist, model, contributing editor and most importantly mother of two, Tabitha is the poster child for those who dream of living and breathing their passions … and she does it with great humility and humanity.

At the outset, she was planning on working as a set design intern at Pinewood Studios. 'I could have had a completely different career, designing film and TV sets. Instead I was pulled in by the fashion world. When I got a styling contract at Calvin Klein, my grandmother asked, "Who's Calvin Klein?"' Tabitha smiles. She soon realized that her passion for shoes was there to stay. 'I'd always had an interest in shoes. When I styled for Calvin Klein and Alexander McQueen, I was obsessed with the process of shoemaking. As a stylist I loved shoes because they would enforce a look and a character.'

Fast-forward, and Tabitha followed her dream. Now based in New York, she is adored by a string of jetsetters, A-listers and editors, as well as by anonymous shoe lovers who have elected with their feet. 'I think it really hit me that I was a shoe designer when I saw girls on the street wearing my shoes,' she says. 'Obviously I'm always honoured when a celebrity wears my creations, or when I've won an award, but seeing a girl on the street wearing my shoes styled in her own look is the biggest compliment I can ever receive.'

She goes on to point out, 'I've been very lucky to have such success from an early stage, with amazing recognition from my peers, but we are a young brand, we have a lot to learn and room to improve.' The industry seems to disagree. In 2009, Tabitha Simmons won the *Footwear News* Launch of the Year, followed in 2011 by the British Fashion Awards Emerging Designer prize. Then in 2012 she was a CFDA/*Vogue* Fashion Fund runner-up. She has since won the CFDA Swarovski Award for Accessories, and was the first winner of the new 'Style Influencer' category at the *Footwear News* Achievement Awards.

Following her instincts has served Tabitha well. Above all, she says, she has the conviction to stand behind her decisions. Also important 'is to have your company and back of house in place'. As she explains, 'You need a strong support group – from manufacturing to shipping to logistics – to run your business and make it successful.'

As for the design process, she is very hands-on, paying attention to every detail. 'I love doing research and visiting vintage shops. There's so much history in the world of design, and it's fascinating to discover new things and different time periods. The creative style of my shoes is primarily English, with a touch of my travels throughout. For instance, my English roots weave their way into all of my collections through corset-like straps, but one season I was inspired by an anniversary trip to Peru and developed a print based on local weaves and fabrics.'

Through four collections a year, Tabitha aims to create designs that are timeless, chic and feminine. Perhaps 'classic with a twist' is the best description.

'I don't like to rush things, so the time necessary to perfect a creation depends on the design,' she explains. 'Since my brand is handmade, we spend a lot of time in the factory in Italy working on the patterns, the grade, the pitch, the fit, and so on. I also like to wear the shoes to test them. The woman who wears my shoes is always on the go and on her feet. It's important to take that into account. I'm always trying to make quality shoes that look and feel great.'

Tabitha aspires to create designs that can be worn season after season, but there is always a little element of difference – an exclusive print, or a special closure. 'I also have two techniques that are signature to my brand,' she states. 'Perforation and broguing. With the first, the fabric is punched throughout with small holes to let the skin or another fabric shine through ever so subtly. With the second, holes are punched into the fabric but selectively rather than throughout, and the punch-outs are in the shape of a heart.'

Another element to receive a recurring starring role in the collections is silk from one of the oldest English mills (it supplied the silk for Princess Diana's wedding dress). This quintessentially British reference appears alongside leathers of the finest quality. Luxury is paired with a slight quirkiness, and finesse is matched with strength, each model having a strong visual identity while being delicate in design. Tabitha's artistic flair shines through (as regards her own taste, she has a passion for Damien Hirst's butterfly paintings and artworks by Dustin Yellin, and she adores the *Predictive Dream* porcelain skull by Katsuyo Aoki that sits in her living room).

If her own patterns are bold, they certainly do not overwhelm. And as with any good design, her creations are inherently tactile. 'My shoes start and end with touch, from selecting fabrics and materials, to producing everything by hand, to the feeling of slipping the shoes on your feet and taking your first steps,' she says. As with everything Tabitha Simmons does, the words 'labour of love' spring to mind.

*www.tabithasimmons.com*

'I work best under pressure. Some people can't take the stress of juggling multiple roles, but I thrive. I think every aspect of my life – from designing to styling to being a mother – strengthens and challenges the other aspects to be the best they can be.'

*(opposite)* Multiple letters of praise and thank you notes addressed to Tabitha and her team: another kind of wall of fame.

*(this page: left column, from top to bottom)* 'Calista' high-heeled open-toe lace-up bootie in black brush-off calfskin, with cut-out details; 'Bryon' biker-style ankle boot in black calfskin, with criss-cross straps and back chain detail; *(centre)* 'Banx' high lace-up round-toe cuissarde boot in black calfskin, with front buckle strap and sculpted skinny heel; 'Alexa' pointy ballerina in black velvet, with crystal panel at toe; *(right)* 'Bailey' stiletto-heeled double-ankle-strap sandal in gold crystal-encrusted satin, with leather accents, grosgrain detailing, back lace-up and slim front buckle strap; 'Phoenix' pointy double-strap ankle boot in Dalmatian-printed suede.

(above) 'Bunny' block-heeled sandal in flamingo pink leather with mini glitter, asymmetric strap, and smooth leather and laser-cut leather accents at vamp with scalloped trim; (left) 'Josephina' high-heeled multi-strap pointy pump in bright butterfly-printed woven satin.

(opposite above) 'Dalia' high-heeled chain-toe perforated and scalloped pump in white calfskin with golden studs; (opposite below) 'Leticia' block-heeled perforated and scalloped ankle-strap sandal in white calfskin.

*(top)* 'Harmony' high-heeled pointy boots in red kidskin suede, with perforated trim and scalloped edge.

*(above)* 'Devon' high-heeled pointy pumps in cream and black brush-off calfskin, with brogue trim.

*(top)* 'Eva' chunky-heeled platform taper-toe boot in white and black calfskin, with wide ankle strap and hook-and-eye front closure.

*(above)* 'Mosshart' high-heeled lace-up ankle boot in oxblood calfskin, with brogue detail and ankle belt.

When Zoe Lee was twelve, she was walking past the Royal College of Art in London with her mother, when the latter said, 'This is probably where you'll go to school when you're older.' The prediction turned out to be absolutely correct. Furthermore, Zoe has remained true to her artistic leanings and only ever worked in fashion. In fact, she got her shoe-designing credentials from none other than the great master, Manolo Blahnik. Establishing her own brand in 2012, she has built a homogenous visual identity that is the envy of many, and the results can be seen in her first stand-alone shop, situated in Le Marais, Paris.

'I do two shoe collections a year, with a few bags,' says Zoe. 'I like collections to develop from one another. I don't do themes, or change my story every season – one story, just perhaps in different languages.' As a result, she produces very small quantities of each style; sometimes only thirteen pairs across all sizes. This explains the high costs of her creations, which she offsets for customers by accepting low margins. 'I find running a small business challenging and often overwhelming,' she admits, 'but the only option is to get on and do it. It takes a long time building something before you can look back and say, "Wow, look at that…" I'm not at that point yet. I hope to be one day, but I'm not in a rush. I feel certain things take time, and this label will be one of those things. I enjoy the process; I'm sure it will only become more complex as time goes on.'

Meanwhile, she designs apparel that is utterly modern thanks to the adoption of futuristic elements – metallic accents, a less-is-more sense of construction, and bespoke lasts and heels. At the same time it is gorgeously historical – giant soft bows billowing on top of leather in the manner of a Louis XIV shoe. All the designs ultimately take a form that is relevant to today, complemented by a muted colour palette. Of her inspiration, Zoe says, 'Usually something will stick in my mind: a picture, an idea, a conversation or a colour. Then I will do a lot of research on material and colour, gather a lot of different things, and then edit with whatever it was that stuck in my mind. At the end of the day I believe a good creation is made by imagination and taste.'

Zoe prefers a shoe that 'enhances rather than creates'. In other words, she aims to provide shoes that contribute to a look, but are not in themselves a loud statement. Desirability and utility blend in harmony. She wears her own shoes all the time, which may be another reason why they seem so in tune with a modern lifestyle. 'The technicalities and logistics involved – from the making of a shoe to how and why it will appeal to the various people I hope it will appeal to – are what give the process purpose and direction, and it's what appeals to me. To create new contexts, through circumstance and situation, in an object such as a shoe is a lot of fun. In fact, I've recently developed a beautiful shoe that will be available exclusively in my shop. I think it's the shoe every woman should have in her wardrobe. It's called the "Soft Lafayette" and it's made from one piece of high-quality kid suede,

with a Bologna construction. The whole shoe is so soft that it folds entirely in half, but retains an elegant shape when on the foot. It's like wearing a feather!' It is clear that Zoe takes pleasure in the hands-on elements of her craft. Blocking, or shaping, leather is a favourite technique. She also carries out a square injection of grey rubber into the sole of every shoe. For brand identification, each pair has a little gold tag.

'I think that fashion is at a bit of a tipping point; that a new direction is coming into view,' she muses. 'We've run out of ways of telling people what to buy. The consumer is researching, learning and incorporating into their life the products they want in a much more sophisticated way. Celebrity endorsement is no longer a good enough reason to buy something. I hope people start to understand more about what they need, be it a luxury or a necessity, and that they start reading products not as "objects of desire" but as "objects for life".'

Zoe's work reconciles the two: desirable objects for life. She recalls a time when a woman came into the shop and told her she couldn't find words to describe how beautiful she thought the shoes were. 'She came in again another day, but I was away,' Zoe recounts, 'so she left a message to say that when she saw the shoes again she felt as if she were in a dream.' An extraordinary emotional response of the kind that will no doubt greet Zoe wherever she goes, as word of her wares spreads around the globe.

*www.zoelee.co.uk*

'Shoes should be as much objects of beauty as products with a use. It is a question of balance: what the shoes were made for, how they aesthetically please the wearer and those around him or her, and the fact that they must carry the wearer through whatever tasks he or she has to do.'

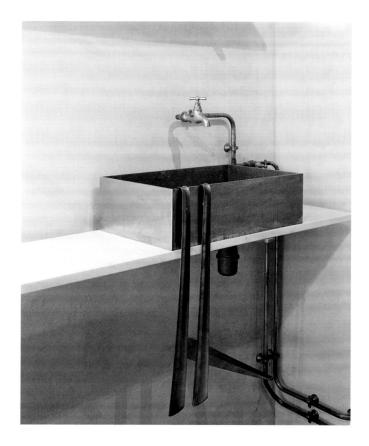

(*this page*) **Zoe Lee's shop and showroom in the very chic rue du Parc Royal is a quintessentially Parisian space, with all its preserved original fixtures: shoe elements blend with the décor, as seen in the elegant brass boot horns suspended from the matching antique sink.**

ART: 28000
COL:

S.I.CERP.
+39 ~~030~~ 0331881098.

ART: ALYA
COL: NERO/BIANCO.

ART: GLADI
COL: NERO.

ART: PIMP.
COL: 439

COPAR.
+39 0444 67 66 54.
ART: AGADIR.
COL: 108

GAIA
ART: PERU
STAMP: ST 237
COL: 8018.

(TRIMS)    FONTANELLA.
029623269.
ART: ARYANNA
COL: 3/0100

ART: ARRIANNA
COL: 1/0101.

(above, clockwise from top left) 'Bonita Silver' mid-heeled d'Orsay pumps in drop pearl print on *crosta* (reversed) leather, with moiré finish on silver calfskin and silver PVC toecap; 'Sun' block-heeled boots in snake-pattern-embossed calfskin, with polyester elastic knit, rubberized calfskin, PVC toecap and silver-plated-effect heel; 'Marlon Grey' mid-heeled pumps in moiré-printed calfskin; 'Marlon Nude' mid-heeled pumps in snake-pattern-embossed calfskin, with grosgrain trim; 'Clinton White' mid-heeled pumps in snake-pattern-embossed calfskin, with rubberized calfskin details; 'Ferriday Grey' Richelieu shoes in lizard-pattern-embossed calfskin, with opaque PVC bow detail.

*(above, clockwise from top left)* '**Ruston**' Richelieu-style d'Orsay shoes in antique gold-finished patent calfskin, with cotton chiffon bow; '**Meraux**' high-heeled d'Orsay pumps in crackled metallic silver calfskin, with T-bar in shape of a bow; '**Roseland**' ankle-strap wedge-style sandals in coated linen and vegetable-tanned calfskin, with gold and white printed calfskin-covered heel and rose gold patent on toe part of insole board; '**Opelousas**' flat ankle boots with bronze-coated linen toe (with plastic overlay toecap), soft translucent white mesh and dot-printed black kidskin suede back, concealed inside zip and white grosgrain trim.

*(opposite, clockwise from top)* '**Mandeville**' d'Orsay flats in embossed nubuck with printed suede calfskin weave; '**Livonia**' flat ankle boots in white flock-printed suede, with white mesh, plastic toe cover, concealed zip and white grosgrain trim; '**Bonita**' high-heeled d'Orsay pumps with embossed nubuck front, printed calfskin heel and back counter, and plastic toe cover; '**Opelousas**' flat ankle boots with bronze-coated linen toe (with plastic overlay toecap), soft translucent white mesh and dot-printed black kidskin suede back, concealed inside zip and white grosgrain trim.

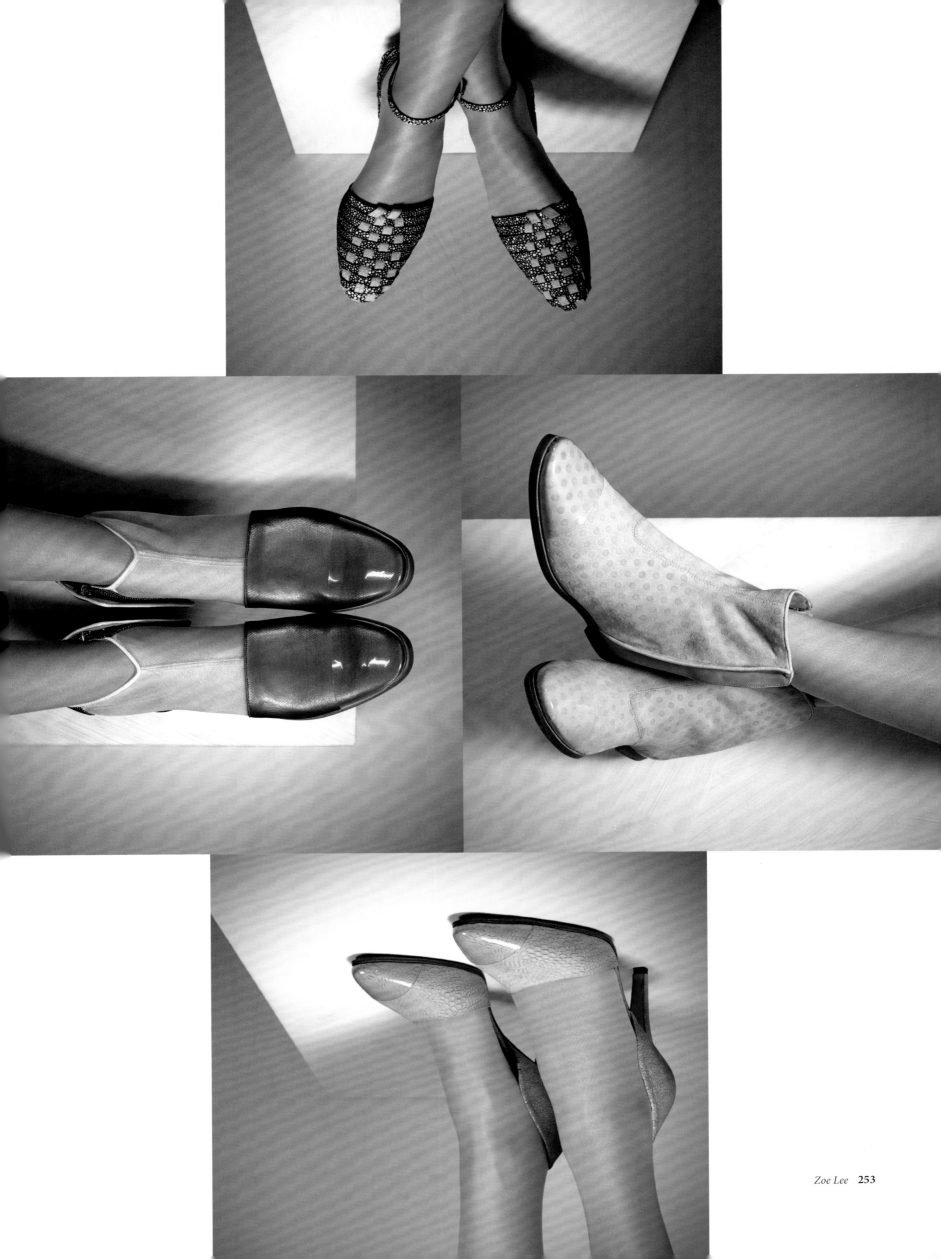

# Picture Credits

Names of collections, information regarding seasons (e.g. Spring/Summer, Fall/Winter) and any other details are as supplied by the designers.

a = above, b = below, c = centre, l = left, r = right, t = top

p. 1 Photo by Sean and Katherine Agger-McMenomy (www.seanmcmenomy.com) // F/W 2013–14.

p. 2 Courtesy of Aperlaï (www.aperlai.com) // 'Geisha Lines', F/W 2014–15.

p. 6 Courtesy of Oscar Tiye (www.oscartiye.com).

**Aga Prus**
p. 8 © Disney 'Minnie: A Style Icon' by Honorata Karapuda (www.honoratakarapuda.com); p. 10 'The Craft of Making Shoes' by Honorata Karapuda (www.honoratakarapuda.com); pp. 11 & 12 (al) Tomasz Pasternak (www.tomaszpasternak.com); pp. 12 (bl) & 13 (al, cr & br) courtesy of Aga Prus (www.agaprus.pl), photography by Tomasz Pasternak (www.tomaszpasternak.com); p. 12 (cr) courtesy of Aga Prus, photography by Honorata Karapuda (www.honoratakarapuda.com); p. 12 (tr) Katarzyna Julia Stach (www.katarzynajulia.tumblr.com); pp. 12 (br) & 13 (tr & cl) courtesy of Aga Prus, photography by Miłosz Paszkowski // p. 11 'Some Things Have a Story to Tell – Stories' collection, F/W 2013–14; p. 12 flat Chelsea boot, 'Some Things Have a Story to Tell – Stories' collection, F/W 2013–14; Derby shoes, 'RR and Aga Prus Take a Walk' collection, S/S 2012; peep-toe sandals, 'Sideways' collection, S/S 2013; p. 13 'Mokasynka', 'Sideways' collection, S/S 2013.

**Alejandro Ingelmo**
p. 14 Jose Marquez (www.marquezphoto.com); p. 16 Lianna Tarantin (www.LiannaTarantin.com); pp. 17, 18, 19, 20 & 21 courtesy of Alejandro Ingelmo (www.alejandroingelmo.com) // p. 17 S/S 2014; p. 18 'Boomerang', F/W 2014–15; 'Cece', F/W 2010–11; 'Mariposa', 'Evening' collection; 'Via Flat', S/S 2012; 'Mariposa', F/W 2013–14; 'Tron', all seasons; p. 19 (a) S/S 2014; p. 19 (b) F/W 2013–14; p. 20 S/S 2013; p. 21 both F/W 2014–15.

**Aleksander Siradekian**
All photos Elizaveta Sharikova // pp. 26 & 27 all F/W 2014–15.

**Allan Baudoin**
pp. 28 & 32 Céleste Dudan (http://celestedudan.tumblr.com); p. 30 (al, ar & br) Jade Nodinot (www.jadenodinot.com); pp. 30 (bl), 31 & 33 Jérôme Darblay // pp. 30 (bl) & 32 (a) shoes commissioned by Ms C.O.J., pp. 31 (l) & 32 (b) commissioned for Ms P.D., p. 31 (r) commissioned by Ms T.B., p. 32 (c) commissioned by Ms C.N. and p. 33 commissioned by Ms L.B.Z., all photographed at the Deyrolle shop, rue du Bac, Paris.

**Amélie Pichard**
p. 34 Boris Camaca (www.boriscamaca.com); p. 36 Stéphane Nauroy (www.canicheabricot.tumblr.com); pp. 37 (original photography), 38, 39 (bl) & 41 (original photography) Nicolas Coulomb (www.nicolascoulomb.com); pp. 39 (ar & br) & 40 courtesy of Amélie Pichard (www.ameliepichard.com) // p. 37 S/S 2014 campaign; pp. 38 & 39 (bl) all F/W 2014–15 campaign; p. 39 (ar & br) F/W 2014–15; p. 40 all S/S 2014; p. 41 S/S 2014 campaign.

**Andreia Chaves**
pp. 42, 44 & 46 courtesy of Andreia Chaves (www.andreiachaves.com); p. 45 & 47 Andrew Bradley (www.andrewbradley.com) // p. 45 2011 launches; p. 46 2014 launches; p. 47 2011 launches.

**Aperlaï**
All photos courtesy of Aperlaï (www.aperlai.com) // p. 52 F/W 2014–15; p. 53 (a) S/S 2015; p. 53 (b) S/S 2014; p. 54 (l) 'Mecano', F/W 2014–15; 'Alana', S/S 2015; 'Memphis', S/S 2014; p. 54 (c) 'Pompom', F/W 2013–14; 'Gatsby', permanent style; 'Pompom', F/W 2014–15; p. 54 (r) 'Mercury Zottsass', S/S 2014; 'Pico Hands', F/W 2013–14; 'Agata Blue Klein', S/S 2015; p. 55 all S/S 2014.

**Aquazzura**
p. 56 Carlo Furgeri (www.carlofurgeri.com); pp. 58–59 courtesy of Aquazzura (www.aquazzura.com); pp. 60, 61, 62, 63, 64 & 65 Hannah Heinrich (www.hannahheinrich.com) // p. 60 F/W 2014–15; p. 61 (a) S/S 2014; p. 61 (b) Cruise 2014; p. 62 F/W 2014–15; p. 63 S/S 2013; p. 64 (t) 'Madison', F/W 2013–14; 'Lola', Pre-Fall 2014–15; p. 64 (c) 'Eagle', F/W 2014–15; 'Belgravia', F/W 2013–14; 'Athena', Cruise 2014; p. 64 (b) 'Eagle', F/W 2014–15; p. 65 (t) 'Tie Me Up', Cruise 2014; 'Charlotte', F/W 2013–14; p. 65 (c) 'Beverly Hills', F/W 2013–14; 'Sexy Thing', F/W 2014–15; 'Xena', S/S 2014; p. 65 (b) 'Venus', Cruise 2014.

**Bruno Bordese**
All photos courtesy of Bruno Bordese (www.brunobordese.com) // p. 69 woven raffia bootie, S/S 2014; woven leather bootie, S/S 2013; wedge sandal, S/S 2015; brogue, S/S 2015; p. 70 punk-inspired boot, F/W 2012–13; high sneaker, S/S 2015; wedge sandal, S/S 2015; p. 71 all S/S 2014; p. 72 both S/S 2014; p. 73 all S/S 2015.

**Burak Uyan**
pp. 74 & 76 Pascal Loperena; all other photos courtesy of Burak Uyan (www.burakuyan.com) // p. 77 all S/S 2011; p. 78 (l) lace-up bootie, F/W 2013–14; ankle boot, F/W 2013–14; high-heeled platform sandal, F/W 2013–14; high-heeled ankle boot, F/W 2011–12; platform sandal, F/W 2011–12; p. 78 (c) all F/W 2013–14; p. 78 (r) all F/W 2013–14; p. 79 (l) ankle-strap sandal, S/S 2012; peep-toe pump, S/S 2012; high-heeled pump, S/S 2014; p. 79 (c) all S/S 2014; p. 79 (r) strappy sandal, S/S 2014; gladiator sandal, S/S 2012; stiletto, S/S 2014; lace-up bootie, S/S 2014; flat sandal, S/S 2014.

**Charline De Luca**
p. 80 Andrea Mete (www.andreamete.com); pp. 82, 83, 84 (r) & 85 courtesy of Charline De Luca (www.charlinedeluca.com); p. 84 (al & bl) Andrea Massari (www.andreamassari.com) // p. 83 (a) 'Regina', F/W 2014–15; 'Riri Fur', F/W 2014–15; 'Michi', carry-over style; p. 83 (b) all S/S 2015; p. 84 both F/W 2014–15; p. 85 S/S 2015.

**Chelsea Paris**
All photos courtesy of Chelsea Paris (www.chelseaparis.com) // p. 89 (l) 'Jasmine', S/S 2014; 'Yemi', S/S 2014; 'Yuwa', S/S 2014; 'Izzy', F/W 2014–15; p. 89 (r) 'Efi', F/W 2013–14; 'Amor', S/S 2014; 'Ada', F/W 2014–15; 'Kinah', Resort 2014; p. 91 'Kimi', F/W 2013–14; 'Yemi', F/W 2013–14; 'Jasmine', F/W 2013–14.

**Diego Dolcini**
p. 92 Milan Vukmirovic; pp. 94, 95, 98 & 99 courtesy of Diego Dolcini (www.diegodolcini.it); pp. 96, 97, 100, 101 & 256 courtesy of Diego Dolcini, photos by Gianluca Pasquini (www.gianlucapasquini.com) // p. 96 (t) 'R32091', F/W 2011–12; 'D36007', F/W 2013–14; p. 96 (c) 'S34022', F/W 2012–13; 'R32029', F/W 2011–12; 'D32090', F/W 2011–12; p. 96 (b) 'S34011', F/W 2012–13; p. 97 (t) 'S34030', F/W 2012–13; 'R32034', F/W 2011–12; p. 97 (c) all F/W 2013–14; p. 97 (b) 'D36005', F/W 2013–14; p. 100 (c) 'S35029', S/S 2013; 'S35009', S/S 2013; 'Z31033', S/S 2011; p. 100 (b) 'DD37006', S/S 2014; p. 101 (t) 'R33060', S/S 2012; 'S35001', S/S 2013; p. 101 (c) 'DD37013', S/S 2014; 'R33001', S/S 2012; 'DD37007', S/S 2014; p. 101 (b) 'Z31017', S/S 2011; p. 256 S/S 2010.

**Edmundo Castillo**
All photos Andrea Barbiroli Photography (www.andreabarbiroli.com) // p. 105 'Kiki', 'American Desert to Palm Beach' collection, S/S 2012; 'Raven', 'Illusion' collection, F/W 2013–14; 'Barbi', 'Warrior' collection, S/S 2014; 'Astrid', 'American Desert to Palm Beach' collection, S/S 2012; 'Mary Jane – I'm Super High', 'Architectural' collection, S/S 2013; 'Amalia', 'Warrior' collection, S/S 2014; p. 108 'Illusion' collection, F/W 2013–14; p. 109 'NYC' collection, F/W 2012–13.

**Ellen Verbeek**
pp. 110, 113, 114 (original photography), 115 (original photography), 116 (original photography) & 117 Stephanie Geerts (www.stefaniegeerts.be); p. 112 Eline Ross // p. 113 (l) 'EV0609', F/W 2009–10; 'EV0109', F/W 2009–10; 'EV1409', F/W 2008–09; p. 113 (c) 'EV0914', F/W 2013–14; 'EV1214', F/W 2013–14; 'EV1809', F/W 2008–09; p. 113 (r) '0112EV', S/S 2012; 'EV1009', F/W 2009–10; 'EV1709', F/W 2008–09; p. 114 S/S 2012; p. 115 S/S 2013; pp. 116 & 117 all S/S 2008.

**Ernesto Esposito**
All photos courtesy of Ernesto Esposito (www.ernestoespositoshoes.com), photos by SIMON Photography (www.simon171.com) // p. 122 (l) slingback pump, S/S 2014; ankle-strap sandal, F/W 2014–15; Richelieu, F/W 2013–14; p. 122 (c) gladiator T-bar sandal, S/S 2014; ankle-strap boot, F/W 2014–15; wedge sandal, S/S 2014; p. 122 (r) ankle sandal, S/S 2014; slingback sandal, S/S 2015; asymmetrical patchwork bootie, F/W 2000–01 and 2014–15; p. 123 F/W 2010–11; p. 124 both S/S 2015; p. 125 (l) 'Hillary' clutch, F/W 2014–15; p. 125 (r) pumps, S/S 2015.

**Fred Marzo**
pp. 126, 128, 131 & 132 (tc, tr & cr) Julien Mingot; pp. 129, 130 & 132 (tl, cl, bl, c, bc & br) Federico Cimatti (www.federicocimatti.com); p. 133 courtesy of Fred Marzo (www.fredmarzo.com) // p. 128 (r) 'Fanny', all seasons; 'Titine', F/W 2013–14; p. 129 'Maguy', S/S 2014; p. 130 all S/S 2014; p. 131 both F/W 2014–15; p. 132 (l) all S/S 2014; p. 132 (c) 'Titop' boot, F/W 2014–15; 'Polly', S/S 2014; 'Titine Wax', S/S 2014; p. 132 (r) 'Titine Top', F/W 2014–15; 'Mado', F/W 2014–15; 'Titine Top', S/S 2014.

**Gio Diev**
p. 134 Laurent Elie Badessi (www.badessi.com); p. 136 courtesy of Gio Diev (www.giodiev.com); pp. 137, 140 & 141 Anton Krustev (www.cvsltd.eu); pp. 138 & 139 Vasil Germanov (www.vasilgermanov.com) // p. 137 (l) 'Fano', F/W 2013–14; 'Atlas', F/W 2012–13; 'Melbourne', S/S 2014; 'Nikko', F/W 2012–13; p. 137 (r) 'Dion', F/W 2013–14; 'Essen', S/S 2015; 'Genova', F/W 2014–15; 'Varna', F/W 2013–14; pp. 138 & 139 S/S 2015 campaign; p. 140 both S/S 2012; p. 141 (a) F/W 2014–15; p. 141 (b) S/S 2015.

**Gordana Dimitrijević**
pp. 142, 146 (original photography) & 147 Julien Mignot (www.julienmignot.com); all other photos courtesy of Gordana Dimitrijević (www.gordanadimitrijevic.fr) // p. 145 (a) 'Ava' bootie, 'Byzantine' collection, F/W 2014–15; 'Enki' bag, 'Fairy Midnight' collection, S/S 2014; p. 145 (b) 'Dita', 'Fairy Midnight' collection, S/S 2014; 'Alex', 'Fairy Midnight' collection, S/S 2014; p. 148 'Ea', 'Beetles Kingdom' collection, F/W 2014–15; 'Alex', 'Byzantine' collection, F/W 2013–14; 'Edgard', 'Beetles Kingdom' collection, F/W 2014–15; 'Alma', 'Fairy Midnight' collection, S/S 2014; p. 149 all 'Fairy Midnight' collection, S/S 2014.

**Isa Tapia**
pp. 150, 152 (tl, cl & bl), 153, 154 & 155 courtesy of Isa Tapia (www.isatapia.com), photos by Isa Wipfli (www.isawipfli.com); p. 152 (ar & br) John M. Langston // p. 153 'Stefania Wave Wedge', Resort 2013; 'Mischa', 'Circus' collection S/S 2014; 'Filipa', S/S 2014; 'Lia', Resort 2013; 'Cha Cha', Resort 2013; 'Nadia', S/S 2014; p. 154 'Circus' collection, S/S 2014; p. 155 'Carmen', Resort 2013; 'Margaret', 'Circus' collection, S/S 2014; 'Cha Cha', Resort 2013.

**Ivy Kirzhner**
All photos courtesy of Ivy Kirzhner (www.ivykirzhner.com) // p. 158 (cl) both F/W 2013–14; pp. 160 & 161 all F/W 2013–14; p. 162 all F/W 2013–14; p. 163 (l) 'Caballero', F/W 2013–14; 'Chevron', F/W 2013–14; 'Pyramid', Pre-S/S 2014; p. 163 (c) 'Roman', S/S 2014; 'Eros', S/S 2014; 'Cavalier', F/W 2013–14; p. 163 (r) 'Vishnu', S/S 2014; 'Caspar', F/W 2013–14; 'Bacchus', S/S 2014.

**Joanne Stoker**
pp. 164, 168, 169 & 171 Sasha Rainbow (www.sasharainbow.com); p. 166 courtesy of Joanne Stoker (www.joannestoker.com); p. 167 courtesy of Joanne Stoker, original photography by Adam Laycock (www.adamlaycock.com); p. 170 Thomas Knights (www.thomasknights.com) and Sasha Rainbow (www.sasharainbow.com) // p. 168 all '1964' collection,

F/W 2014–15; p. 169 all '1941' collection, S/S 2014; p. 171 both 'Indian Artisan Summer' collection, S/S 2012.

**Kerrie Luft**
pp. 172 & 179 courtesy of Kerrie Luft, photos by Cristina Capucci (www.cristinacapucci.com); pp. 174, 175, 176, 177 & 178 courtesy of Kerrie Luft (www.kerrieluft.com) // all classic styles with no specific season; 'Thandie' and 'Carine' in permanent collections.

**Laurence Dacade**
p. 180 Eric Guillemain (www.2bmanagement.com); pp. 182 & 183 courtesy of Laurence Dacade (www.laurence-dacade.com); p. 184 Frédéric David; pp. 185, 186 & 187 Thomas Kletecka // p. 184 (a) both F/W 2013–14; p. 184 (b) Pre-Fall 2014–15; p. 185 (l) 'Gwen', F/W 2014–15; 'Heidi', S/S 2015; 'Herlin', S/S 2015; p. 185 (c) both F/W 2014–15; p. 185 (r) 'Merli Brodé', S/S 2014; 'Hilde', S/S 2015; 'Helie', S/S 2015; pp. 186 & 187 all S/S 2015.

**Oscar Tiye**
p. 188 Giuseppe Toja (www.nitrox.it/f.php?f=8); pp. 190, 191, 192 & 193 courtesy of Oscar Tiye (www.oscartiye.com) // p. 192 (l) 'Malikah', F/W 2013–14; 'Jamila', S/S 2014; 'Cleopatra', S/S 2014; p. 192 (c) 'Jamila', S/S 2014; 'Malikah', F/W 2014–15; 'Minnie', F/W 2014–15; p. 192 (r) all S/S 2014; p. 193 (l) 'Minnie', F/W 2014–15; 'Minnie', F/W 2014–15; 'Yumna', S/S 2015; p. 193 (c) 'Minnie', F/W 2014–15; 'Malikah', F/W 2014–15; 'Abal', S/S 2015; p. 193 (r) 'Raisa', S/S 2015; 'Amira', F/W 2014–15; 'Casandra', F/W 2013–14;

**Paul Andrew**
All photos courtesy of Paul Andrew (www.paulandrew.com) // p. 198 (l) 'Aristata', S/S 2014; 'Shirin', Pre-Fall 2014–15; 'Zenadia', F/W 2014–15; p. 198 (r) 'Shakti Soir', Resort 2014; 'Lexington', Pre-Spring 2015; 'Artemis', S/S 2014; p. 199 (l) 'Passion', Pre-Spring 2014; 'Taos', Pre-Fall 2014–15; 'Nya', Pre-Spring 2014; p. 199 (r) 'Zenadia', Pre-Fall 2014–15; 'Tempest', Pre-Spring 2015; 'Tigrado', Pre-Fall 2014–15; p. 202 Pre-Spring 2015; p. 203 Pre-Spring 2014.

**Rupert Sanderson**
pp. 204, 207 (original photography) & 211 (original photography) Eddie Wrey; pp. 206, 209 & 210 courtesy of Rupert Sanderson (www.rupertsanderson.com); p. 208 Mary Fellowes (www.maryfellowes.com) // p. 207 S/S 2014 campaign; p. 208 F/W 2011–12 campaign; p. 209 (l) 'Zandy', S/S 2013; 'Ohio', S/S 2014; p. 209 (c) 'Bignor', S/S 2014; 'Estelle', Resort 2009 (iconic style); 'Mitzy', Resort 2014; p. 209 (r) 'Elba', Resort 2003 (best-selling pumps); 'Harting', S/S 2013; 'Lintie', Resort 2012; p. 210 'Wilson', F/W 2014–15; 'Tweeny', F/W 2014–15; 'Marshal', F/W 2014–15; 'Gretel', Pre-Fall 2014–15; 'Frances', F/W 2014–15; 'Grenade', Pre-Fall 2014–15; 'Isolde', Pre-Fall 2014–15; 'Salome', F/W 2014–15; 'Urania', F/W 2014–15; p. 211 F/W 2013–14 campaign.

**Simona Vanth**
pp. 212, 215, 216, 217, 218 & 219 Dario Salamone Photography (www.dariosalamone.com); p. 214 courtesy of Simona Vanth (http://simonavanth.tumblr.com) // p. 215 all 'Boldrini Lady' collection, S/S 2014; pp. 216 & 217 'Concrete Island' collection, F/W 2013–14; p. 218 'Primitive Plastique' collection, S/S 2012; p. 219 all 'Androids Fan Club' collection, F/W 2014–15.

**Sophia Webster**
All photos courtesy of Sophia Webster (www.sophiawebster.com) // p. 223 (a) 'Marissa', F/W 2014–15; p. 223 (b) 'Riko', Pre-Fall 2014–15; pp. 224 & 225 all F/W 2014–15; pp. 226, 227 & 228 all S/S 2014; p. 229 F/W 2014–15 campaign.

**Suecomma Bonnie**
pp. 230, 232, 233, 236 & 237 courtesy of Suecomma Bonnie (www.suecommabonnie.com); pp. 234 & 235 Ahn Joo Young (www.agencyteo.com) // p. 233 (l) platform bootie, S/S 2010; flat slingback sandal, 'Unique Sportism' collection, S/S 2015; high-heeled ankle boot, S/S 2010; p. 233 (c) high-heeled bootie, S/S 2010; 'Climbi in Green' walking boot, 'Walking in the Forest' collection, F/W 2014–15; high-heeled sandal, 'Unique Sportism' collection, S/S 2015; p. 233 (r) 'Climbi in Gold' walking boot, 'Walking in the Forest' collection, F/W 2014–15; peep-toe ankle boot, 'Unique Sportism' collection, S/S 2015; high-heeled bootie, S/S 2010; pp. 234 & 235 all 'Glam, Sporty and Mix' collection, S/S 2014; p. 236 both 'Unique Sportism' collection, S/S 2015.

**Tabitha Simmons**
p. 238 courtesy of Tabitha Simmons (www.tabithasimmons.com), photo by Steven Pan (www.stevenpan.com); all other photos courtesy of Tabitha Simmons // p. 241 (l) both F/W 2014–15; p. 241 (c) 'Banx', F/W 2014–15; 'Alexa', F/W 2013–14; p. 241 (r) both Resort 2014; pp. 242 & 243 all S/S 2014; p. 244 (a) 'Harmony', F/W 2013–14; p. 244 (b) 'Devon', F/W 2014–15; p. 245 (a) 'Eva', F/W 2011–12; p. 245 (b) 'Mosshart', F/W 2014–15.

**Zoe Lee**
p. 246 Charlie Wheeler (www.charliewheeler.co.uk); pp. 249, 251 & 252 courtesy of Zoe Lee (www.zoelee.co.uk); pp. 248 & 253 (t, l & r) by Alexander Guirkinger (www.aleguirk.com); pp. 250 & 253 (b) Sean and Katherine Agger-McMenomy (www.seanmcmenomy.com) // p. 250 'Homer', F/W 2013–14; p. 251 all F/W 2014–15; pp. 252 & 253 all S/S 2014.

p. 256 Photo courtesy of Diego Dolcini (www.diegodolcini.it), photo by Gianluca Pasquini (www.gianlucapasquini.com) // S/S 2010.

# ACKNOWLEDGMENTS

Dear designers, it has been a joy to collaborate with you, and your creations have kept me inspired and in elegant company day after day, so: *tout simplement, merci.*

Thank you also to everyone who helped me liaise with the talented names featured in this book – Caroline Allen, Andrea Barbiroli, Courtney Bennett, Samantha Carrepani, Joe Chang, Emily Dantonio, Casey Dworkin, Ricardo D'Almeida Figueiredo, Francesca Guardavaglia, Rosanna Hill, Kim Jooha, John M. Langston, Chase Leger, Lara Lucas, Patrick McGregor, Chiara Pierro, Flavia Roncolato, Hélène Rossignol, Claudia Stokes, Cho Sunghoon, Roberta Tacchini, Federica Taveggia, Nishant Vajpayee, Giorgia Viola and Meghan Wood – and to all the photographers: you deserve my full gratitude.

A special mention to Tatiana Verstraeten (www.tatianaverstraeten.com), Kimberlin Brown (www.kimberlinbrownjewelry.com), Richard Nahem (www.ipreferparis.net), Nicky Elder (http://purplepr.com) and Roxanne Robinson-Escriout (www.wwd.com) for their kind support in activating their networks.

To my publisher, Thames & Hudson: this is book number six and must surely correspond to an anniversary of some kind! To the graphic design duo whose creative skills have no limit: Amélie Bonhomme & Amy Preston, there are no words to say how much I admire your work.

*(right)* 'Lady Chain' high-heeled multi-strap sandal in metallic calfskin and satin in various colours, with Swarovski crystals and metal chain, by Diego Dolcini.